Cambridge Elements

Elements in Politics and Communication
edited by
Stuart Soroka
University of California, Los Angeles

CATCHING FIRE IN THE NEWS

The Necessary Conditions for Media Storms

Amber E. Boydstun
University of California, Davis

Jill R. Laufer
University of California Center Sacramento

Dallas Card
University of Michigan

Noah A. Smith
University of Washington

Shaftesbury Road, Cambridge CB2 8EA, United Kingdom

One Liberty Plaza, 20th Floor, New York, NY 10006, USA

477 Williamstown Road, Port Melbourne, VIC 3207, Australia

314–321, 3rd Floor, Plot 3, Splendor Forum, Jasola District Centre, New Delhi – 110025, India

103 Penang Road, #05–06/07, Visioncrest Commercial, Singapore 238467

Cambridge University Press is part of Cambridge University Press & Assessment, a department of the University of Cambridge.

We share the University's mission to contribute to society through the pursuit of education, learning and research at the highest international levels of excellence.

www.cambridge.org
Information on this title: www.cambridge.org/9781009498418
DOI: 10.1017/9781009498432

© Amber E. Boydstun, Jill R. Laufer, Dallas Card, and Noah A. Smith 2026

This publication is in copyright. Subject to statutory exception and to the provisions of relevant collective licensing agreements, with the exception of the Creative Commons version the link for which is provided below, no reproduction of any part may take place without the written permission of Cambridge University Press & Assessment.

An online version of this work is published at doi.org/10.1017/9781009498432 under a Creative Commons Open Access license CC-BY-ND 4.0 which permits re-use, distribution and reproduction in any medium providing appropriate credit to the original work is given. You may not distribute derivative works without permission. To view a copy of this license, visit https://creativecommons.org/licenses/by-nd/4.0

When citing this work, please include a reference to the DOI 10.1017/9781009498432

First published 2026

A catalogue record for this publication is available from the British Library

ISBN 978-1-009-49841-8 Hardback
ISBN 978-1-009-49844-9 Paperback
ISSN 2633-9897 (online)
ISSN 2633-9889 (print)

Additional resources for this publication at www.Cambridge.org/Boydstun

Cambridge University Press & Assessment has no responsibility for the persistence or accuracy of URLs for external or third-party internet websites referred to in this publication and does not guarantee that any content on such websites is, or will remain, accurate or appropriate.

For EU product safety concerns, contact us at Calle de José Abascal, 56, 1°, 28003 Madrid, Spain, or email eugpsr@cambridge.org

Catching Fire in the News

The Necessary Conditions for Media Storms

Elements in Politics and Communication

DOI: 10.1017/9781009498432
First published online: January 2026

Amber E. Boydstun
University of California, Davis

Jill R. Laufer
University of California Center Sacramento

Dallas Card
University of Michigan

Noah A. Smith
University of Washington

Author for correspondence: Amber E. Boydstun, aboydstun@ucdavis.edu

Abstract: Why do some events catch fire in the news, producing a media storm, while many similar events go all but unnoticed? This Element uses a fire triangle analogy to explain the necessary conditions of media storms. The "heat" is the spark: a dramatic event or discovery. The "fuel" is the political and cultural landscape, including similar items in recent news, and current debates that allow the event to be framed in a resonant way. The "oxygen" is the available news agenda space, plus attention the event receives beyond the news (by activists, politicians, people on social media, etc.). Media storms are not easily predictable; it takes the right event, at the right time, with the right momentum of attention. But when the political stars align and a media storm erupts, it can be a window of opportunity for change. This Element is also available as Open Access on Cambridge Core.

This Element also has a video abstract:
www.cambridge.org/EPCM_Boydstun_abstract

Keywords: media storms, news coverage, news values, journalistic gatekeeping, police use of force

© Amber E. Boydstun, Jill R. Laufer, Dallas Card, and Noah A. Smith 2026

ISBNs: 9781009498418 (HB), 9781009498449 (PB), 9781009498432 (OC)
ISSNs: 2633-9897 (online), 2633-9889 (print)

Contents

1 Introduction — 1

2 What We Know About Media Storms — 6

3 Methodology: Identifying the Correlates of Media Storms — 14

4 The Fire Triangle Model of Media Storms — 18

5 The Role of Political Actors in the Fire Triangle Model — 31

6 Necessary Elements of Media Storms: Heat, Fuel, and Oxygen — 40

7 Effects of Media Storms — 62

References — 76

An online supplementary material is available at www.Cambridge.org/Boydstun

1 Introduction

It seems like there's a kind of national conversation going on right now about those who are paid to protect us, who sometimes end up inflicting lethal harm upon us. But for me, this conversation is old, and I'm sure for many of you the conversation is quite old. It's the cameras that are new. It's not the violence that's new.
– Ta-Nehesi Coates, author of *Between the World and Me* (Goodman 2015)

In 2014, and again in 2020, US news media lurched their attention to the issue of police use of deadly force, specifically against unarmed Black people. A count of *New York Times* articles, for example, shows that in the decade before 2014, news coverage of the issue was consistently low, averaging just over 100 articles per year. In August 2014, however, coverage surged following the death of Michael Brown, an unarmed Black eighteen-year-old man who was shot and killed by a police officer in Ferguson, MO, and whose body was left uncovered in the street for hours. The *New York Times* published 179 articles related to police use of deadly force that month alone, and 705 articles in total that year. Coverage in the *Times* and other news outlets stayed high for a couple years but then declined to pre-2014 levels. In 2020, though, coverage spiked again following the gruesome murder of George Floyd, a forty-six-year-old unarmed Black man killed in Minneapolis, MN, on May 25 as a police officer kneeled on his neck for nearly nine minutes, while bystanders watched. In June 2020 alone, the *Times* article count was 860, with 1,525 articles that year. Both Michael Brown's and George Floyd's stories were instances of what past work has labeled "media storms," formally defined as a sudden, high-level surge of news coverage for at least a week, but better understood as the type of news coverage around an item that is so sudden and so pervasive that even people not paying attention to the news have heard about the story.

The much lower levels of news coverage about police use of deadly force in the time periods before, between, and after the media storms surrounding Michael Brown's and George Floyd's deaths did not mean there were fewer people (or fewer Black people) in the US being killed by police in those periods. Although perfect data on lethal police encounters do not exist, available data collected by the Fatal Encounters collective[1] and *The Washington Post*[2] suggest that more than 1,000 people are killed in America each year during encounters with police – with Black people representing a near-consistent 25% of the fatalities. (Accounting for overall representation in the US, Black people are 3.23 times more likely to be killed by police compared to White people (Schwartz and Jahn 2020)). Since 2010 specifically, the estimated yearly

---
[1] https://fatalencounters.org/.
[2] www.washingtonpost.com/graphics/investigations/police-shootings-database/.

number of people killed by police has varied from about 1,300 to 2,100, with Black people representing 27% of these fatalities.[3] Together, these statistics suggest that each week of low media coverage hides a week in which, on average, police in the US kill between six and eleven Black people.

In this way, news media not only reflect reality but also shape our perception of it. Although it is impossible for news outlets to cover all the policy problems in the world all the time, in moments when an ongoing problem fails to make the news, this inattention is a form of misrepresentation. As Lawrence says, the news media capture "an arena of struggle over the meaning of events, the existence of problems, and the search for solutions" (2022: 23). Thus, when a media storm *does* erupt, it shines a spotlight on an otherwise underattended problem.

Yet despite the significance of media storms, no research to date has identified the precise factors needed to prompt a media storm. For example, Michael Brown and George Floyd became household names because of the media storms that followed their deaths. But if their deaths did not mark any changes in the underlying problem of police use of deadly force, then why did their deaths spark media storms when so many other cases do not? Put more broadly, what conditions are required for a media storm to occur?

This question is important because media storms are important. When a media storm is underway, the news agendas of various news outlets become more congruent, sending people a more unified signal about what to pay attention to (Gruszczynski 2020). This unified signal is effective. For instance, news coverage has a statistically stronger effect on Congressional attention when that coverage occurs as part of a media storm (Walgrave et al. 2017). And anecdotally, there is much evidence to suggest that media storms can serve as windows of opportunity for societal change. As just one example of many, consider the media storm surrounding the sexual abuse of children by Catholic priests and the church's systemic cover-up of these instances of abuse. This media storm was initiated by a series of *Boston Globe* articles published in 2002, following months of investigative journalism. Of the thousands of cases of alleged sexual assault by Catholic priests in the US in the preceding four decades, less than 0.5% occurred in 2002 (the year the story broke). Yet 32% of the survivors of these abuses came forward in 2002 during, and in the wake of, the media storm (Boydstun 2013). This data point suggests that by highlighting the underlying problem of sexual assault at such a high volume of attention, the media storm helped destigmatize the act of making an allegation, thereby encouraging more survivors to come forward. Increased allegations

---

[3] https://fatalencounters.org/.

acted as a catalyst for policy changes, which in turn prompted more media coverage, creating a positive feedback loop of media attention and societal change. Because media storms are important, it is important to understand when and why they happen.

In this Element, we investigate the conditions that tend to mark, perhaps even portend, a media storm. From these markers, we can infer a set of necessary conditions under which a media storm will erupt. We use a mixed-methods approach, starting with a rich set of eighty-six in-depth case studies of events that did (and didn't) become media storms in policy areas spanning police use of deadly force to water quality, immigration policy to airplane safety, and many more in between. Quantitative analysis allows us to validate which items were media storms and which were not, and qualitative analysis allows us to identify the common factors that differentiate events that became media storms from those that did not. We do not offer a predictive model of media storms here, per se; indeed, our conclusion is that they are largely unpredictable because their component parts are so hard to control or anticipate. Rather, we identify the correlates of media storms – the combination of factors that are collectively present in the case of media storms and not collectively present when media storms do not materialize. The result is a theorized set of conditions that are necessary for a media storm to occur.

We develop and apply our model in the context of national media storms in the US news media, as an important example of a competitive media marketplace. Yet we hope our model will be useful in other contexts as well (see our discussion on Media Storms of Different Scope in Section 2). Media storms are phenomena familiar to anyone living in a democratic media system – and probably nondemocratic media systems, too. Examples from other nations include, in Portugal, the 2007 disappearance of three-year-old Madeleine McCann from a holiday apartment where she was staying with her family while on vacation from England, with the McCann family serving as a Patient Zero target of widespread trolling on the newly released Twitter social media platform, then just a year old; in Germany, the 2016 New Year's Eve sexual assaults in Cologne and other cities, with this media storm prompting the German Parliament to pass the "No Means No" law that among other things lowered the bar of non-consent from actively defending oneself to verbally saying "no" and made it easier to deport a migrant convicted of a sex crime; and in the UK, the 2020/2021 "partygate" scandal about government and Conservative Party gatherings in violation of COVID-19 pandemic restrictions, with this media storm adding to the forces that prompted the then prime minister Boris Johnson to resign. Understanding the necessary conditions of media storms is important in every geographical and political context. As we discuss in Section 7, we expect our model would apply comparatively, at least to other democratic media systems, although with key conditioning factors such as the competitiveness of the media system and the party structure of the government.

In Section 2, we give more definition to and background about the concept of "media storms." In Section 3, we recount the methods we used to identify the factors that demarcate events that prompt media storms from those that do not. We then turn to our main discussion in Sections 4–6, where we use fire as an analogy to discuss the three core elements that we argue are necessary conditions for media storms.[4] In the case of real fires, the "fire triangle" is a simple model designed to help the average person understand the conditions needed to create most fires, and its most well-known application is in the prevention of wildfires (Ballard et al. 2012). The fire triangle is made up of three ingredients: heat, fuel, and oxygen (Bear 2019).[5] We borrow this triangle imagery to offer a model of the ingredients needed to trigger media storms (as illustrated in Figure 1): the "heat" of the newsworthiness of an event, the "fuel" of historical and current political landscape against which that event is (or is not) relevant and cognitively accessible, and the "oxygen" of available media agenda space as well as amplifying attention the event receives beyond the traditional news media (e.g., from politicians and the public).[6] We posit that only a news item that has high levels of all three ingredients will prompt a media storm.[7] In other words, *strong levels of heat, fuel, and oxygen are individually necessary conditions on their own, but only in combination are they jointly sufficient to prompt a media storm*. Finally, in Section 7, we close by highlighting some of the very real effects of media storms on public opinion and public policy in recent years, underscoring the importance of understanding the necessary conditions of future media storms.

In short, we argue that media storms are not easily predictable; it is not simply the case that when an extraordinary event occurs, media respond with extraordinary levels of coverage. Media storms also do not simply happen; they are the product of human beings – news editors, news consumers, policymakers, policy

---

[4] We use the analogy of fire with sharp awareness of the power of actual fire, as evidenced by the increasing frequency of devastating fires in urban and suburban neighborhoods, including in the Los Angeles, California, area in early 2025.

[5] Lifelong goal of citing Smokey Bear in an academic text, achieved.

[6] We were tempted to rebrand the term "media storm" as "media firestorm" to reflect our model. We resisted this temptation, both because a change in terminology could further confuse an already jargon-heavy literature and because in the world of literal fires, the term "firestorm" refers to the rare phenomenon whereby the heat from a fire creates its own wind system – a process even more complex than the analogy of catching fire that we employ (although we return to this concept in discussing the 2025 media storm surrounding President Trump's tariffs).

[7] Although there may be historical cases where strong levels of all three elements did *not* lead to a media storm, we have been unable to find them.

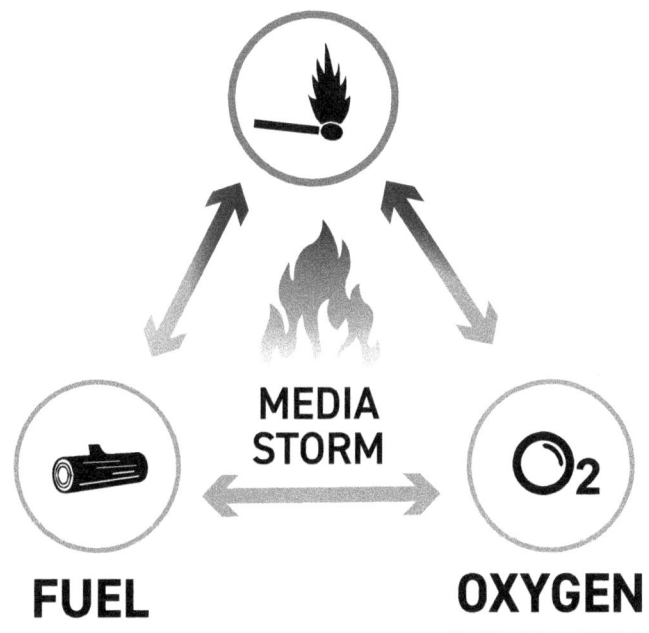

Figure 1 The media storm fire triangle model

activists, and many others – making decisions about which events and issues to prioritize. The result of this complex system of human attention allocation is that media storms occur only when (1) the right event (i.e., perceived to be highly newsworthy) occurs, (2) at the right time (when there is available media agenda space and when previous and current items in the news offer the story a relevant hook), and (3) gets talked about by the right people (amplifying the story beyond the mainstream news). But when the political stars align and a media storm erupts, it can prompt lasting effects, establishing a new media equilibrium – and, often, a new policy equilibrium – that will likely hold until the next media storm in that policy space occurs.

2 What We Know About Media Storms

Before we turn to addressing our core question about the necessary conditions of media storms, we need to lay some groundwork for the concept of media storms and how they arise from the journalistic news generation process. Let's start with the definition. Boydstun, Hardy, and Walgrave define a "media storm" as "a sudden surge in news coverage of an item, producing high attention for a sustained period" (2014: 509). Their concept of a media storm builds on prior work surrounding media dynamics, including examination of "media hypes," which are functionally synonymous with "media storms" (e.g., Vasterman 2005; Wien and Elmelund-Præstekær 2009). In essence, media storms are instances where a key event occurs in such a way as to draw competing and imitating coverage from multiple news organizations, becoming a "self-reinforcing news wave" (Vasterman 2005). This line of research is unified by the core phenomenon of news coverage exploding around an unfolding news item, such that the average person in that news market is aware of the item even if they themselves are not carefully tracking the news.

Empirically, Boydstun, Hardy, and Walgrave (2014) define a media storm as occurring when news coverage of an item meets three criteria: (1) a sudden surge in news coverage, (2) at a very high level, (3) lasting for at least a week.[8] In addition to these three criteria, they posit a fourth criterion, saying, "we conceptualize true media storms as being those that meet our three formal criteria and that register as such across multiple news outlets in a given media

---

[8] Specifically, Boydstun, Hardy, and Walgrave (2014) use the following criteria: (1) the level of coverage needs to have increased by at least 150% from the previous week (i.e., more than double last week's coverage), (2) the underlying event needs to be high enough so that the larger issue area it belongs to consumes at least 20% of the media agenda space, and (3) the high level of coverage needs to last for at least seven days. As we discuss in the section on scope later in Section 2, these criteria can be adjusted to fit different research questions and datasets, so long as the measurement decisions adhere to the core notion of a media storm.

system" (2014: 512). True media storms at the national level, then, are those that erupt, in part, from competing news outlets clamoring to get the next fresh take on an unfolding storyline. In practice, it appears that most, if not all, events that reach media storm status in one national news outlet also satisfy this fourth criterion of capturing the attention of multiple outlets. For example, Litterer, Jurgens, and Card (2023) find that the mean number of US news outlets covering a typical storm was seventy-six (the median was seventy-four). One inference from this finding is that, at least in terms of national news outlets, a media storm that erupts in one news outlet is almost certainly erupting across that portion of the media ecosystem.

Importantly, media storms do not just happen. As we will discuss more in Section 5, media storms are the results of political actors of many stripes making decisions about how to spend their attention.

How Do Media Storms Unfold?

Although research to date does not identify the specific conditions under which a media storm is likely to erupt, past work does offer insight into the dynamic patterns observed in media storms as they unfold, as well as the journalistic mechanisms that underly them. Scholars have discussed the notion of media storm dynamics (although not by that name) for decades. For example, we know that some policy problems tend to follow what Downs (1972) calls the "issue attention cycle."[9] For these problems, attention cycles through different phases: first, a period of little or no attention to the policy problem, even though the problem is ongoing and in need of attention; second, a sudden discovery of the problem by the media and the public, accompanied by a sense of urgency to address it; third, a realization of how complex and hard to solve the problem is; fourth, a gradual decline in public interest in the problem; and fifth, a period of "post-problem" inattention that feeds back into the first stage of the next cycle. Other work adds texture to the notion of an issue attention cycle. Whereas Downs talks about the second stage of the cycle as a period of positive enthusiastic problem-solving, for instance, Schattschneider (1960) talks about the kind of cases where the sudden "discovery" of a problem is met with a more negative, accusation-based form of urgency.

Common across these and other scholars is the notion that the public agenda, the media agenda, and the policymaking agenda all move through cycles of

---

[9] Downs explains that the policy problems that tend to go through the issue attention cycle have three characteristics: first, the problem disproportionately affects a numerical minority of the population; second, the problem is generated by social arrangements that benefit a numerical majority (or powerful minority) of the population; and third, that the issue lacks "intrinsically exciting qualities" (Downs 1972).

attention to ongoing policy problems. In each case, it takes a confluence of multiple forces to produce major agenda overhaul. Focusing on the policy-making process, Kingdon offers a "multiple streams" model to explain the interconnected factors that need to align in order for policy change to occur. He explains that a "window of opportunity" for policy change to occur opens only when a policy problem (1) is identified and defined as a problem by the media, citizens, issue groups, and so on (the "problem stream"), and (2) potential policy solutions are proposed (the "policy stream"), (3) in the context of a hospitable political climate (the "politics stream"). One key contribution of Kingdon's policy streams model, also consistent with past research on media attention, is that eruptions of policy change and media attention are highly serendipitous, and thus very difficult to predict.

Past research also reveals several things about the nature and dynamics of media storms once they begin. For example, examining front-page coverage of the *New York Times* in the US and *De Standaard* in Belgium, Boydstun, Hardy, and Walgrave (2014) show that media storm coverage is a fundamentally different kind of dynamic species than non-storm coverage. As predicted by the punctuated equilibrium model of policy agenda dynamics (Baumgartner and Jones 2009), non-storm news coverage moves in fits and starts, fluctuating between almost no change (equilibria) and sudden but short-lived bursts of change (punctuations). But media storm coverage is quite different. Unlike other bursts of change, media storms, by definition, erupt into a much higher level of news coverage and last for a longer period. But, once in storm mode, media attention tends to change much more gradually, fluctuating moderately around the high level of attention before dying down more slowly than the staccato of non-storm punctuations (Litterer, Jurgens, and Card 2023).

The pattern by which media storms erupt matches the power law dynamics of other tipping point scenarios in the context of complex systems, including avalanches, financial crashes, and fashion fads (Granovetter 1978). In these scenarios and in the case of media storms, a series of independent but mutually reinforcing factors combine to build momentum, increasing the likelihood that the next action will be one that reinforces rather than counteracts the trend. The result in the case of a media storm tends to be an initial low level of news coverage that suddenly surges into a flurry of attention before gradually dying back down.

As for the duration of media storms, Litterer, Jurgens, and Card (2023) find that the typical media storm peaks quite early (in the first few days), and then declines gradually over time, usually lasting at least two weeks both in terms of total amount of coverage and in the number of outlets covering it each day. They find this pattern to be especially true for storms precipitated by unexpected events, such as a celebrity death. At the same time, a subset of media storms in their study were more predictable, such as the outcome of a court trial, where there was much more news coverage laying the groundwork in anticipation of the main event, resulting in a more gradual incline in coverage.

Media storm dynamics are born in part through journalistic patterns of news coverage. Boydstun (2013) explains how media storms erupt within the "police" model of news generation coined by earlier authors (e.g., Bennett 2003; Zaller 2003). Table 1 summarizes Boydstun's alarm/patrol hybrid model of news generation. News outlets often operate in "patrol" mode, whereby for any "neighborhood" surrounding a given issue or topic (e.g., immigration, crime, health care, sports, weather patterns, etc.) reporters assigned to that beat drive up and down the figurative streets of that neighborhood and report on anything important they find. At other times, news outlets operate in "alarm" mode, waiting back at the figurative police station until a major event, a whistleblower, or something else triggers an "alarm" that alerts them to a newsworthy item. Of course, there are many one-off stories that result from neither one of these styles of reporting. But of key interest here, media storms (highlighted in the top-left quadrant of Table 1) occur when journalists shift from alarm mode to patrol mode, or vice versa. For example, in 2005 news outlets raced to cover the alarm of Hurricane Katrina but then shifted into patrol mode, in many cases embedding reporters in the area for weeks. In patrol mode, these reporters investigated back-alley items such as racial inequities in housing and inefficiencies in FEMA's administration. These patrol-based stories helped to amplify and sustain news coverage following the hurricane, producing the high and prolonged coverage necessary to qualify as a media storm (Haider-Markel, Delehanty, and Beverlin 2007).

An example of the flip case, where news outlets move from patrol mode to alarm mode, was the aforementioned Catholic priest abuse scandal. The scandal broke not because of any sudden "alarm" event but rather because journalists at the *Boston Globe* (specifically the Spotlight team of journalists, highlighted in the 2015 movie of the same name) had spent months patrolling the figurative neighborhood of allegations of sexual abuse by Catholic priests and indications of institutional-level coverup by the Catholic church, before publishing their findings in a series of news articles. These news articles, in turn, served as an alarm for the rest of the media system, and other news outlets raced to cover the story, prompting a media storm (Boydstun 2013). Thus, the alarm/patrol hybrid model helps explain the journalistic forces that combine to produce media storms.

Table 1 A typology of news-generation modes and the types of news coverage that result as presented in Boydstun (2013: 65)

	Alarm mode (where news outlets rush to cover a hot new story)	**Non-alarm mode**
Patrol mode (where news outlets dig into the details of a story, looking for new aspects of the story to uncover)	*Resulting type of news coverage* **Media storm:** A sudden surge of news coverage at a high level for at least a week *Example news items* 9/11 terrorist attacks Hurricane Katrina Catholic priest abuse scandal Trayvon Martin's shooting Global pandemic George Floyd's murder Jan 6, 2021 insurrection at the US Capitol	*Resulting type of news coverage* Low-level sustained coverage or high-level sustained coverage *Example news items* Ongoing military action overseas Olympics General weather patterns General presidential elections
Non-patrol mode	*Resulting type of news coverage* A momentary media surge in news coverage but not at a high enough level and/or for long enough to qualify as a media storm *Example news items* Haiti earthquake Michael Jackson's death	*Resulting type of news coverage* Low-level coverage for a brief period *Example news items* Human interest stories Most crimes

Media Storms of Different Scope

Past empirical work on media storms has been conducted mostly within the specific parameters of individual national news outlets (e.g., the *New York Times*). But past research also makes clear that the concept of media storms could be studied in contexts that might encourage researchers to adjust one or more of these parameters (i.e., expanding beyond a single source, shifting from a national level to a different level, and/or considering sources beyond traditional news). We mention these three parameters in the hopes that readers will keep them in mind in the sections that follow as we examine the necessary conditions of media storms. Whether the established findings about media storms – including those we present here – would apply under different parameter definitions of a media storm is an open question, one we invite the reader to consider.

First, media storms could be studied across the scope of a news media marketplace. That is, scholars could expand their definition of media storms to those news items that meet the three criteria from Boydstun, Hardy, and Walgrave (2014) – a sudden increase in attention, a very high level of attention, and lasting for an extended time – *and* their fourth criterion of needing to meet these three thresholds across a certain number of news sources. The true notion of a media storm, as we and other scholars have envisioned it, is a dramatic surge in coverage that ripples through the entire national news media marketplace (and beyond). Again, work by Litterer, Jurgens, and Card (2023) suggests that a media storm in one national news outlet generally means a media storm across news outlets nationwide. In the case study findings we introduce in Section 3 and discuss in Section 6, we use data from the five most prominent US newspapers (*Chicago Tribune, Los Angeles Times, New York Times, The Wall Street Journal*, and *The Washington Post*), and each case that met our criteria of a media storm overall also presented as a media storm within each of the five outlets. While we expect that the findings we present here would hold in a broader study that encapsulates the entire national marketplace (newspapers, magazines, TV, radio), we cannot know for sure.

Second, although media storms as defined by Boydstun, Hardy, and Walgrave (2014) are those instances where *national* media coverage explodes around a news item, the concept of media storms could be applied geographically either more broadly or more narrowly – or to non-geographic spaces, such as a Reddit community. For example, the 2023 escalation of the conflict between Israel and Hamas likely met the criteria of a media storm as on a global scale. Other examples of global media storms might include the reactor explosion at the Chernobyl nuclear power plant in Ukraine in 1986 or the 9/11 terrorist attacks in the US in 2001. Yet, to date, no studies of media storms have used as an empirical criterion the spread of the story across news media marketplaces around the world. There is important work, however, on the phenomenon of a media storm that begins local and spreads across a national media marketplace; Usher and Hagman (2025) provide a meticulous case study of the media storm that began local but then caught fire nationally surrounding Darren Bailey, a Republican Illinois State Senator who in 2020 sued the Illinois Governor for the stay-at-home order put in place during the pandemic. At the other end of the geographical spectrum, no scholarship that we know of has examined the questions of media storms we tackle here from an exclusively local perspective, focused on media storms that erupt at (but stay within) the local or regional level.[10] Such an approach would be useful in examining the dynamic news signals that people in a particular area receive. In addition to knowing about any national (and global) media storms that occur, people are also aware – perhaps even more acutely aware – of media storms at the local level, for example involving local government scandal, a contentious local election, the firing of a beloved high school principal, and so on. In the spring of 2023, for example, the close-knit community of Davis, CA, was jolted by a string of stabbing attacks that killed two beloved members of the community and severely wounded a third. Few people outside of Davis would have heard this news (which received a single article in the *New York Times*), but the stabbings certainly caused a media storm in the local media system, occupying near-daily headline space in the local and regional newspapers and on the regional network television stations, as well as in local groups on social media networks like Nextdoor and Facebook. In the case of global and local media storms (as well as media storms in a non-geographic space), we have no strong theoretical grounding on which to assume that existing research about media storms would (or would not) apply. The theories and findings we put forward here might generalize to these other contexts, but they also might not, underscoring the importance of future work in these areas.

Third, the established work on media storms treats social media coverage as positive feedback for traditional news coverage and thus defines media storms strictly in terms of newspaper, television, and online (e.g., Politico.com) *journalism-based* coverage of a news item. Following this line of conceptualization, in this Element we categorize social media coverage as part of the "oxygen" required to ignite and sustain a media storm in mainstream news. But the concept of a media storm can be applied to social media itself, with attention on social media being the primary phenomenon of interest and attention in

---

[10] Although see von Sikorski's (2017) research on regional media storms in the context of scandals.

mainstream news helping to amplify it (Vasterman et al. 2018). As a whimsical example, in 2015 a picture of a striped dress went viral on social media, with people divided in their perceptions of whether the colors of the dress were black and blue or white and gold. This debate spilled over into traditional news as well, with sources like the *New York Times* publishing stories first about the social media buzz and then follow-up articles such as science-based reporting explaining the difference in color perceptions (Fleur 2015), but it failed to become a media storm in the traditional news. Yet it undoubtedly constituted a media storm in the context of social media. Future research could include or focus exclusively on media storms that erupt on social media, whether or not they also meet the criteria of a media storm in the traditional news. Another question for future research is whether less serious media storms that erupt on social media, such as "the dress" debate in 2015, or the "Barbenheimer" trend of pairing the Barbie and Oppenheimer movies in the summer of 2023, are more likely to occur when there is a lull in the traditional news cycle. Again, we don't necessarily expect that the established findings (including those we present here) would hold if applied to media storms on social media.

In all the potential modifications we have discussed here, and in others we have not explicitly called out, we can imagine researchers making theory-driven decisions to adjust the empirical criteria of a media storm as needed for different contexts.

Media Storms Matter

Finally, we know from past research that media storms matter. Using Google search data, for example, Boydstun, Hardy, and Walgrave (2014) show that the public pays quick attention and a lot of it – to news items at the heart of media storms, compared to paying much less (if any) attention to news items that, while substantively similar, do not erupt into media storms. In follow up work, Walgrave and colleagues (2017) show that a one-story increase in news coverage around a policy issue has a significantly stronger effect on Congressional attention to that issue if the story occurs as part of a media storm rather than outside of a storm. And a key finding from research on agenda setting (including from Schattschneider (1960) and Downs (1972), mentioned earlier) is that when media and public attention turns to an issue, even a short period of high attention can be enough to produce some kind of change, akin to Kingdon's "windows of opportunity" in the policy realm (2010).

In the case of news coverage, media storms indeed provide "windows of opportunity" for changes in public opinion, policy, and cultural norms, as we discuss more in Section 7. These windows of opportunity are likely facilitated not only by the sheer volume of news coverage during a media storm but also because of the aforementioned finding from Gruszczynski (2020) that during a media storm the individual news agenda of outlets across the media system become more congruent. Another mechanism that might help pry open these windows is *how* news outlets talk about, or frame, an event or issue while in media storm mode. For instance, Baumgartner, De Boef, and Boydstun (2008) document the dramatic shift in media framing of the death penalty that occurred during media storms in the 1990s, changing from a predominant narrative of crime and punishment to one of fairness and innocence. This finding suggests that media storms coincide with changes in issue framing, as news outlets clamor to establish fresh perspectives and angles on the same topic in a competitive news marketplace, thereby expanding the norms of how that issue is discussed.

In thinking about the effects of media storms, it is important to note that events that ignite a media storm are not always spontaneous or "accidental," as in the case of most media attention around the issue of police use of deadly force (Lawrence 2022). Many media storm events are "institutional," coordinated by political elites as planned or staged events. Examples of these types of media storm events are UN climate speeches from important leaders or arguments in front of the Supreme Court. However, the accidental or spontaneous events can disrupt news outlets' status quo and make even bigger waves than the anticipated events, reshaping journalistic patterns in the process. As Lawrence writes, "some accidental events become the centerpieces of struggles to designate and define public problems, as other groups vie to provide journalists with frames and claims to define these events. As journalists try to make sense of troubling news events, news routines may extend to underutilized news sources and marginalized perspectives" (Lawrence 2022: 22).

Although these findings help us understand what media storms are, how and why they unfold, and what effects they can have, the question remains: What are the conditions needed to prompt a media storm in the first place? Is the media landscape a "survival of the fittest" environment, where the events that trigger media storms are simply the most newsworthy items? Or is there more involved?

3 Methodology: Identifying the Correlates of Media Storms

Previous scholarship has laid strong groundwork for exploring how and when societal problems come to be spotlighted in the news. In a parallel to the George Floyd case, Lawrence (2022) examines the media storm surrounding the 1991 brutal beating of Rodney King by police, juxtaposing other contemporary cases that received little or no media coverage. Lawrence explains that journalists covering these stories act as "mediators" in their choice of stories to focus on, and she links these decisions to the considerable constraints that govern and generally limit media coverage of police use of force. Informational constraints, in particular, can be mitigated when video of the incident is available, as when a bystander on a balcony videotaped police officers brutally beating Rodney King (Lawrence 2022).

In this light, part of the explanation of why one event or story gets highlighted above others might seem obvious. In the case of George Floyd's murder, bystander Darnella Frazier used her cellphone to capture video of the shocking cruelty of a White police officer kneeling on Floyd's neck for eight minutes and forty-six seconds as Floyd struggled to breathe, called out to his deceased mother, and ultimately lost consciousness and died (Arango, Dewan, and Bogel-Burroughs 2021). In Michael Brown's case, however, there was no video. This discrepancy alone suggests that the explanation of why some events catch the media's attention, while others don't, is more complex than the event itself or even the presence or absence of graphic video evidence.

What, then, are the conditions of, or surrounding, an event that tend to herald a media storm? We tackled this question using a mixed methodological approach. We started by examining a massive original dataset of two decades' worth of news coverage of six policy issues (capital punishment, climate change, gun control, immigration, same-sex marriage, and smoking/tobacco) that we compiled for a different project, totaling some 100,000 news articles (Card et al. 2015). Using this dataset, we identified all media storms using three quantitative criteria in line with past research: an increase in coverage of at least 150%, occupying a large portion of the media agenda,[11] and maintaining that level of coverage for at least a week. As for the fourth criterion (coverage across multiple news outlets), in practice every one of the media storms we identified using the other three criteria also met this fourth criterion, with high levels of coverage spanning the different news outlets in the dataset. In all, across twenty years of news coverage of six different issues, these criteria yielded forty-four media storms. A qualitative deep dive revealed that many of these storms surrounded events that were predictably newsworthy (e.g., the Sandy Hook Elementary School shooting in 2012), but it also revealed other events that in isolation were not nearly as newsworthy, at least at a national level (e.g., state

---

[11] Boydstun, Hardy, and Walgrave (2014) set the criterion for a "large portion of the media agenda" as an issue area capturing 20% of the given media agenda. Lacking an accurate measurement of the full size of the media agenda of interest, we operationalized the volume criterion for this project as an article count of at least four standard deviations more than the mean article count for that issue across the entire dataset.

legislative efforts to pass new gun control laws in Connecticut). These qualitative findings offered face validity to the idea that the newsworthiness of an event is not alone sufficient to predict whether a media storm will occur.

Next, we employed the help of many thoughtful and talented undergraduate research assistants with a diverse array of background experiences to identify and compare events that *prompted* media storms with comparable events that did *not* prompt media storms. We used the following structured methodology:

1. We started by brainstorming major news items that seemed *likely* to have met the empirical criteria of a media storm (a sudden surge in coverage, at a very high level, lasting for at least a week), based on internet searching as well as our own memories and conversations with others. We were careful in this stage not to share with the research team the list of verified media storms from the earlier dataset of news coverage across six issues, but the team brainstormed several media storms that were also included in that list. The result of this brainstorming process: eighty-one potential media storm events.

    To check whether each potential media storm met the quantitative criteria, we used the ProQuest US Major Dailies archive, which chronicles coverage (including online coverage) from five major US newspapers (*Chicago Tribune, Los Angeles Times, New York Times, The Wall Street Journal*, and *The Washington Post*). We applied the established criterion of a sudden increase in attention (Boydstun, Hardy, and Walgrave 2014) by requiring an increase in coverage of 150% or more from the pre-storm week to the week where the candidate storm erupted. For the second criterion of a high volume of coverage, we required the first week of the storm to have at least 100 news articles (meaning roughly 3 articles a day, on average, for *each* of the five major national newspapers in the database).[12] For the duration criterion, we required that the level of coverage stay high throughout at least the first week. Again, in practice, all items that met these three media storm criteria also met the fourth, with high levels of coverage across the news outlets in the US Major Dailies archive. Our online appendix contains the keyword search strings we used. Of the eighty-one potential media storms we had brainstormed, seventy-five turned out to satisfy the quantitative media storm criteria.

---

[12] Since we are focused here on news coverage of specific events rather than entire issue areas, we use a threshold of 100 articles rather than the 20% of agenda space used by Boydstun, Hardy, and Walgrave (2014). We view 100 articles as a resonable event-level threshold to parallel the 20%-of-agenda issue-level threshold.

2. For each validated media storm event, we did our best to find a parallel event with roughly the same qualitative characteristics as the media storm event but where we estimated the parallel event did *not* become a media storm – a task akin to finding the dog that did not bark. Some storms (e.g., the terrorist attacks of September 11, 2001, or the 2020 global pandemic) were so unparalleled that there simply was no counterpart non-storm event in the modern era. Other cases were difficult to pair for other reasons. For instance, Rose McGowan had long voiced to friends her account of being sexually assaulted by Harvey Weinstein but did not make her accusations public until 2017 when the #MeToo media storm ignited around sexual assault and harassment. We simply could not find a parallel non-storm event (i.e., a celebrity of McGowan's status making public accusations of sexual assault before the #MeToo movement took off), presumably because prior to the #MeToo movement, even celebrities of her status did not risk making public accusations. Of the seventy-five verified media storm events, we were able to match forty-three with parallel non-storm counterparts (eighty-six events in all).
3. For each media storm and non-storm event, we qualitatively evaluated and then documented the attributes of the event itself, as well as the surrounding context. This lengthy list of events and their attributes revealed three conditions, or elements, that were consistently present to a strong degree in the case of every media storm, but at least one of which was weak or missing from each non-storm event. We label these three elements "heat," "fuel," and "oxygen," as described more in Sections 4–6.
4. For each storm and non-storm event, we rated the event according to each element (heat, fuel, and oxygen) from Very Low to Very High based on comprehensive research, including reading news articles, social media posts, and Google Trends data, where applicable.

   - **Heat:** The newsworthiness of the event, including factors like scope of impact, shock value, and availability of evidence.
   - **Fuel:** The historical and current political, cultural, and economic context that amplifies the event's relevance.
   - **Oxygen:** The amount of available media agenda space, as well as attention and amplification from beyond traditional news sources, such as social media, politicians, and activist groups.

While our decisions about how high or low each element was in each case are inherently subjective, we used a set of guidelines to standardize our categorizations (see online appendix). For example, for the heat of an event to be rated as "Very High," the event needed to have a high degree of newsworthiness (see

Sidebar in the Section 6, Heat) *and* compelling photographic/video evidence to assist in virality. "Very High" fuel required that the event be one that was already salient for the average American *and* could be easily framed in a way to hook into a salient touchpoint. "Very High" oxygen required available media agenda space (i.e., the absence of a major competing media storm) *and* significant amplification of the event by at least three distinct types of non-news sources (e.g., celebrities, politicians, state or federal legislation, international organizations, public protests, viral hashtags, etc.), such that an average person not tuned into the traditional news but paying attention to other channels of communication like social media would likely hear about it.

Our online appendix showcases eighteen of these pairs of media storm versus non-storm events (labeled in each header with the year it was most prominent in the news), with categorizations and brief descriptions of the heat, fuel, and oxygen for each, along with the following empirics:

- The week of the highest level of news coverage for the event
- Number of news stories in the week prior to the week of highest coverage
- Number of news stories in the week of highest coverage
- Number of news stories in the month of highest coverage

We also describe key outcomes (e.g., policy shifts) that occurred at least in part because of the media storm within each pair. We feature four of these eighteen comparisons in Figure 2 (Israel–Hamas war versus Sudan war), Figure 3 (Greta Thunberg versus Mari Copeny), Figure 4 (H.R. 4437 versus Secure Fence Act), and Figure 5 (Titan submersible disaster versus Messenia migrant disaster).

Readers may surely quibble with some of the subjective evaluations we have made in selecting and categorizing the items in each comparison. We welcome these quibbles as part of the valuable discourse to be gained by applying our theoretical fire triangle model to very real items in the news.

4 The Fire Triangle Model of Media Storms

The research process described in the previous section allows us to see the observed correlates of media storms versus non-media storms. In every case of a confirmed media storm we examined, there were three conditions – *heat*, *fuel*, and *oxygen* – that were present at strong levels (specifically, a categorization of "High" or "Very High" according to our guidelines; see online appendix). And in every case of a parallel event that did *not* become a media storm, at least one of these conditions was weak or lacking (a categorization of "Medium Low" or lower). Based on these correlates, we offer a theoretical model of the necessary

Israel-Hamas War (2023)

(In the News: 10/2023 – present)   Media Storm? **YES**

Week of highest news coverage: October 9–15, 2023
Number of news articles week before: 110
Number of news articles that week: 1,000
Number of news articles during peak month coverage: 3,180

On October 7, 2023, Hamas launched a surprise attack on Israel, killing nearly 1,200 people and taking 251 hostages. Israel responded with intense retaliation, including airstrikes on Gaza. As of 2025, nearly 70,000 people have been killed in the war according to the Gaza Health Ministry and Israeli Ministry of Health, and two-thirds of the buildings have been destroyed. Israel has also cut off water, food, fuel, and electricity to Gaza, exacerbating a severe humanitarian crisis. There has been massive internal displacement, spilled over into neighboring Lebanon, and escalated fighting with Hezbollah, despite numerous failed intervention attempts to end the violence.

HEAT — VERY HIGH
- The October 7, 2023, Hamas attacks were shocking, involving high numbers of casualties, sexual violence, home invasions, and an attack on a music festival, with the hostage situations amplifying the emotional toll.
- The attacks were well documented, with thousands of violent and graphic images quickly circulating online. The subsequent war in Gaza has produced gripping images, including of destroyed buildings and starving children.
- The attacks and ensuing war also tap into long-standing American values of combating antisemitism.

FUEL — VERY HIGH
- The conflict is contextualized by well-known and significant historical events, starting with the creation of the state of Israel in 1948—an event in which the U.S. played a significant role.
- Conflicts between Israel and Hamas have persisted throughout the 20th and 21st centuries, with frequent clashes.
- The current war is thus set against longstanding tensions in the Middle East that are well known, if not well understood, among Western audiences.

OXYGEN — VERY HIGH
- Beginning in 2024 across the U.S., college students staged protests, walkouts, and encampments, mostly in support for Palestinians. In Spring 2024, violence erupted at encampments at Columbia and UCLA, drawing heavy criticism for police interventions that left some students severely injured.
- Congress held a series of hearings on antisemitism and the campus protests, calling university presidents from Rutgers, Northwestern, UCLA, and others to testify.
- Activists have enacted consumer boycotts targeting Israeli imports and American companies, like Starbucks and McDonald's, for their perceived support of Israel.

OUTCOMES RELATED TO THE ISRAEL-HAMAS WAR MEDIA STORM:
- **Politics:** The war was a significant topic in the 2024 U.S. election, highlighting divisions between and within political parties. Some analysts believe media attention hurt the chances of Josh Shapiro, the governor of Pennsylvania and staunch supporter of Israel, from becoming Kamala Harris's VP nominee. Early election postmortems posit that some voters in Michigan also voted against the Democrats because of the division.
- **Protest Responses:** To control protest activity, many universities created new, stricter policies regarding campus access, student conduct, and encampments.

Figure 2 Israel–Hamas war versus Sudan war

Sudan War (2023)

(In the News: 4/2023 – present) Media Storm? **NO**

Week of highest news coverage: April 15-21, 2023
Number of news articles week before: 4
Number of news articles that week: 93
Number of news articles during peak month coverage: 213

On April 15, 2023, a civil war broke out between the Sudanese Armed Forces and the Rapid Support Forces in Sudan. The conflict has devastated Sudan and neighboring countries. As of 2025, this conflict has caused over 150,000 deaths in Sudan. Additionally, over a third of the country's population, 18 million people, face hunger and starvation following widespread famines, and over 11 million have been displaced within Sudan as the country continues to descend into cycles of violence, often along ethnic lines.

- The Sudanese conflict has been deadly and devastating, with the UN calling it "one of the worst humanitarian nightmares in recent history." Reports include sexual violence, ethnic killings, and a cholera surge, with over 80% of hospitals out of service.
- Unlike the Israel-Hamas war, there has been low circulation of the relatively scarce video and photo evidence from the war. This lack of documentation lowers the shock value and emotional engagement of the war in the news.
- This war is occurring in a North African country that is culturally less familiar to Americans than Israel and Gaza, lowering the perceived newsworthiness of the conflict.

HEAT: MEDIUM

- Previous civil wars in Sudan serve as potential fuel; 200,000 civilians died between 2003 and 2005 in what the U.S. Secretary of State called a genocide.
- Yet, while there was conflict in Sudan for decades before this war, the conflict did not make a lasting impression on the Western media and public.
- Western audiences in general lack an understanding of the historical context of the conflicts in Sudan.

FUEL: LOW

- This conflict has been less controversial in the U.S. than the Israel-Hamas war, making it less of a political priority overall and essentially absent from the 2024 U.S. election.
- Other governments have been involved in this war; notably, Egypt and Saudi Arabia have assisted the Sudanese Armed Forces, and the UAE has financially supported the Rapid Support Forces. The U.S. government has also been somewhat involved in negotiations, but news coverage of these efforts has been minimal.
- The war has garnered minimal social media activism and protests.

OXYGEN: MED. LOW

OUTCOMES RELATED TO THE **ISRAEL-HAMAS WAR MEDIA STORM:**

Columbia canceled Spring 2024 commencement, while USC barred its valedictorian from speaking.
- **University Resignations:** In large part as a result of the media coverage surrounding the Congressional hearings, Harvard University President Claudine Gay and Columbia University President Minouche Shafik both resigned.
- **Boycotts:** Boycotts contributed to a nearly $12 billion drop in value for Starbucks in a single month, and McDonalds likewise experienced a slowdown in sales.

Figure 2 (cont.)

Greta Thunberg (2019)

(In the News: 2018 – present) Media Storm? **YES**

Week of highest news coverage: September 20–26, 2019
Number of news articles week before: 38
Number of news articles that week: 144
Number of news articles during peak month coverage: 230

In 2018, when she was 15, Greta Thunberg started skipping school to protest outside the Swedish Parliament, calling for more government action on climate change. Her climate activism gained global attention, sparking a worldwide movement. Thunberg was named *Time* magazine's Person of the Year in 2019 and has been nominated multiple times for a Nobel Peace Prize.

HEAT
- Thunberg is a citizen of a wealthy, white nation (Sweden), lending her perceived credibility and newsworthiness. [VERY HIGH]
- She introduced an unconventional approach to messaging for a teenage activist, including sharp and angry criticism of world leaders (e.g., "how dare you") on the international stage.
- Her captivating actions to lessen her carbon footprint were captured in photos and video footage, including traveling to speak at the UN in 2019 via a two-week journey across the Atlantic on a small, carbon-neutral racing yacht.

FUEL
- Her activism began at a time of increasing youth political engagement (e.g., the *March for Our Lives* movement organized by teenage survivors of the 2018 mass school shooting in Parkland, FL), giving traction to her activism. [VERY HIGH]
- The urgency of her cause was amplified by a lack of strong climate leadership and a solidifying scientific consensus about the climate crisis.
- Worsening natural disasters in the news added to the existential threat of climate change.

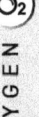

OXYGEN
- She effectively engaged with critics (e.g., Donald Trump), using irreverent social media posts that often went viral across media platforms. [VERY HIGH]
- World leaders amplified her story (e.g., inviting her to speak at the 2018 United Nations Climate Change Conference).
- Her strong social media presence amplified her reach and influence, with her Twitter follower count growing from 400,000 to over 3 million by the end of 2019.

OUTCOMES RELATED TO THE **GRETA THUNBERG MEDIA STORM**:

- **Global Climate Strikes:** Thunberg inspired millions to join the *Fridays for Future* movement, pressuring governments on climate issues.
- **Youth Mobilization:** More broadly, she empowered a new generation of youth activists to advocate for environmental change.
- **Increased Climate Change Awareness:** She amplified the visibility of the global conversation, pushing climate change to the front of many government and

Figure 3 Greta Thunberg versus Mari Copeny

Mari Copeny (2016)
(In the News: 2016)   Media Storm? **NO**

Week of highest news coverage: May 1-7, 2016
Number of news articles week before: 0
Number of news articles that week: 7
Number of news articles during peak month coverage: 7

In April 2016, Amariyanna "Mari" Copeny (Little Miss Flint) wrote a message to President Obama about the ongoing lead water crisis in Flint, Michigan. Obama responded by visiting Flint in May 2016 and approved $170 million in relief at the end of the year. Copeny continued her activism focused on the water crisis, including crowdfunding enough money for over 1 million bottles of water for Flint residents.

- Copeny was newsworthy for how young she was at the time (8 years old), but the newsworthiness cards were stacked against her as a Black person trying to draw attention to Flint's predominantly low-income, Black community.
- There were no viral images or videos from Copeny's activism.
- Although more than 100,000 people in Flint were exposed to elevated lead levels, the population affected was restricted to that area.

HEAT

- Her activism started during a period of lower youth activism (e.g., before the *March for Our Lives* movement).
- The intersection of race and environmental issues was not yet a major topic on the federal agenda, making it hard for Copeny's activism to fit into a broader political narrative.
- The local nature of the Flint water problem made it hard to link in with broader conversations, such as about climate change.

FUEL

- In 2016, President Obama responded to Copeny's letter and visited Flint, Michigan.
- However, most of the oxygen was centered on the water crisis itself [see Figure 6], and very little was devoted to Copeny specifically; while Copeny was surely a contributor to the media storm surrounding the crisis, she did not become the central focus or largest voice of the media storm.
- Although Copeny built a social media presence (including nearly 150,000 Twitter followers), it never gained the same level of traction as Thunberg's.

OXYGEN

OUTCOMES RELATED TO THE **GRETA THUNBERG MEDIA STORM**:

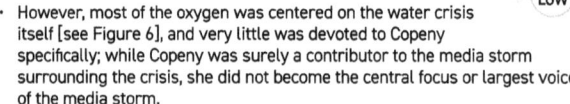

policy-oriented group agendas.
- **Political Influence:** Some governments, especially in Europe (e.g., Finland), declared climate emergencies and strengthened policies in the wake of her activism.
- **Policy Impact:** Her efforts contributed to initiatives like the European Green Deal aimed at carbon neutrality by 2050.

Figure 3 (cont.)

H.R. 4437 (2006)

(In the News: 2005 – 2006)   Media Storm? **YES**

Week of highest news coverage: May 20–26, 2006
Number of news articles week before: 89
Number of news articles that week: 124
Number of news articles during peak month coverage: 294

On December 16, 2005, the Border Protection, Antiterrorism, and Illegal Immigration Control Act of 2005 (H.R. 4437) passed the U.S. House by a 57% majority. It required harsher penalties for undocumented immigration, requiring immigration officials to deport any suspected undocumented immigrant within 100 miles of the border without due process; requiring employers to check employees' citizen status and criminalizing businesses that would not comply; and making it a crime to assist an "illegal alien" to remain in the U.S. The bill expired at the end of the congressional session with no Senate vote and provoked delayed but widespread protests. These protests, in turn, prompted a media storm in the spring of 2006.

HEAT
- The bill was inherently newsworthy for the harshness of its policies.
- It was also highly partisan; 88% of House Republicans supported it, while 81% of Democrats opposed it.
- The resulting protests in 2006 were newsworthy because they were widespread and had a clear message (e.g., on May 1 organizers used the slogan "A Day Without an Immigrant" to mobilize an immigrant work boycott to draw attention to their contributions).

FUEL
- From 1990 to 2007, the U.S. experienced a spike in immigration, from 3.5 to 12 million unauthorized immigrants with many efforts at reforms and enforcement on the federal and state levels.
- Notable previous policy initiatives included CA Prop 187 in 1994 and President Clinton blocking all immigrants from receiving healthcare and social services in 1996 (both later reversed by the courts).
- The 9/11 terrorist attacks of 2001 had adverse effects on how all immigrants were viewed in the U.S., heightening xenophobia.

OXYGEN
- Citizen activism mobilized hundreds of protests across 39 states, culminating on May 1, 2006, when about a million people, mostly of Latino descent, conducted a general strike ("A Day Without an Immigrant").
- Activist and advocacy groups like the ACLU and Human Rights Watch heavily criticized the bill.
- Protests sparked backlash from conservative politicians, like Pat Buchanan, and comments from President Bush and other politicians, including the future presidential candidate Barack Obama, who supported the protests.

OUTCOMES RELATED TO THE H.R. 4437 MEDIA STORM:
- **Blocked Policy** *(the bill did not pass the Senate):* Widespread protests and grassroots efforts helped prevent the Senate from voting on the bill.
- **New Policy** *(a milder bill passed soon thereafter):* The Secure Fence Act (the non-media storm in this comparison) was signed into law in 2006 with little fanfare and most of the stricter regulations around immigration dropped; the bill was framed less in terms of criminalizing immigration and more in terms of national security.
- **Voting Patterns Changed:** Arguably influenced by this media storm, two-thirds of Hispanic voters voted for Democratic candidates in the 2006 midterms, whereas in

Figure 4 H.R. 4437 versus Secure Fence Act

Secure Fence Act (2006)
(In the News: 2006)   Media Storm? **NO**

Week of highest news coverage: July 15-21, 2006
Number of news articles week before: 2
Number of news articles that week: 7
Number of news articles during peak month coverage: 12

Less than a year after H.R. 4437 passed the House and barely five months after the widespread protests, the Secure Fence Act (H.R. 6061) passed Congress and was signed into law by President George W. Bush on October 26, 2006. The Act directed the Secretary of Homeland Security to install two layers of secure fencing at the U.S.–Mexico border, as well as new surveillance technology to ensure there would be fewer, if any, illegal border crossings. The fencing would stretch nearly 700 miles across the border.

- The idea of a 700-mile-long border fence was inherently newsworthy, being both interesting and confounding.
- Unlike H.R. 4437, the Secure Fence Act made it to the president's desk and was signed into law.
- This bill had no policies that heightened the risk of deportation for U.S. residents; the fact that this bill focused more on border security than on direct policing and deportation of immigrants made it less newsworthy.

 MEDIUM HEAT

- The same immigration debates and legislation that served as fuel for H.R. 4437 also worked as fuel for the Secure Fence Act.
- Yet attention fatigue following the spring protests likely dulled the role of fuel in this case.
- Small segments of fencing were built on the southern border by previous administrations, like *Operation Gatekeeper* under the Clinton administration, which saw the construction of fencing at one of the busiest border crossing points: the San Diego-Tijuana border.

 HIGH FUEL

- Whereas H.R. 4437 received a lot of attention from multiple advocacy groups opining on the bill's potential to cause harm, the Secure Fence Act did not receive this attention.
- There were no widespread protests or demonstrations against H.R. 6061.
- Likewise, there was relatively little public discussion about the policy by politicians.

 LOW O₂ OXYGEN

OUTCOMES RELATED TO THE H.R. 4437 MEDIA STORM:

2000 41% of Hispanic voters had voted for President Bush. In 2008 this number increased further, with 73% of Hispanics voting for President Obama, a trend which endured until the presidential election of 2024.

- **Rise of Latino/a as a Political Identity:** The protests framed immigrant rights through the lens of workers' rights, human rights, and civil rights, helping to forge a more politically cohesive identity for the diverse population of Latino/as in America, with two-thirds of Latino/as surveyed reporting that they believed the 2006 marches represented a new U.S. social movement.

Figure 4 (cont.)

Titan Submersible Disaster (2023)

(In the News: 2023 – 2024)   Media Storm? **YES**

Week of highest news coverage: June 20–26, 2023
Number of news articles week before: 6
Number of news articles that week: 231
Number of news articles during peak month coverage: 281

On June 18, 2023, the Titan submersible, a small submarine privately operated by OceanGate, was lost at sea during a 5-person mission to observe the remains of the Titanic in the North Atlantic Ocean. A media storm erupted almost immediately, as the public became real-time spectators of a suspenseful search-and-rescue mission that gave hourly updates. The search cost the U.S. alone $1.2 million. Four days later, it was determined that the Titan had imploded, killing all onboard: the CEO, a billionaire, a renowned explorer, and a father-son pair. A dual U.S.–Canadian investigation followed, with many questioning the safety of such future excursions.

HEAT   VERY HIGH
- The small number of passengers aboard the vessel meant that followers of the story could learn their names and their personal stories. This increased the heat, as did the fact that all the passengers were wealthy and from Europe.
- The search for the Titan included videos of helicopters scanning the ocean's surface, photos of search-and-rescue crews, and eventually, photos of the remains of the Titan.
- The sinking of the Titanic is a legendary event imprinted on Western minds, making this story more newsworthy.

FUEL   HIGH
- The limits of where tourists can travel were being stretched prior to the Titan's disappearance, including director James Cameron's descent to the deepest point on the ocean floor in 2012, and Jeff Bezos's space trip in 2021.
- The Titanic's sinking over 100 years prior, and its legacy in Western pop culture, acted as fuel by giving this story a recognizable face.
- Audiences were accustomed to narratives about hoped-for rescues of small groups like miners in a collapsed mine in Chile in 2010 and a youth soccer team in a cave in Thailand in 2018.

OXYGEN   VERY HIGH
- The search-and-rescue mission was a dual-nation effort, with the Canadian Coast Guard, the U.S. Navy, and the U.S. Coast Guard leading the search.
- Social media was flooded with content about the missing submersible, with influencers following the story and reporting to followers both during and after the implosion became known.
- Stories arose about prior OceanGate safety concerns, with one former employee alleging being fired for raising safety concerns about the submersible.

OUTCOMES RELATED TO THE TITAN SUBMERSIBLE MEDIA STORM:

- **Federal Investigation and Hearings:** Over a 15-month period, the National Transportation Safety Board released several reports, and the U.S. Coast Guard called 24 witnesses for a live-streamed public hearing. The Coast Guard's final report, released August 5, 2025, faulted OceanGate for the implosion and outlined 17 corporate, federal, and international practice and policy recommendations. Results from the U.S. Attorney's Office investigation are still pending.
- **Call for Regulatory Changes:** Federal investigations revealed regulatory and

Figure 5 Titan submersible disaster versus Messenia migrant disaster

Messenia Migrant Boat Disaster (2023)
(In the News: 2023)

Media Storm? **NO**

Week of highest news coverage: July 1–July 7, 2023
Number of news articles week before: 0
Number of news articles that week: 9
Number of news articles during peak month coverage: 14

Just four days before the Titan submersible failed to resurface, a large fishing boat (the Adriana) capsized 45 miles off the coast of Greece. Despite its intended capacity of 400 people, the Adriana was carrying an estimated 750 Pakistani, Syrian, Egyptian, and Palestinian refugees and migrants, traveling from Libya to Italy. It capsized during its voyage, on June 14, 2023, with rescued survivors taken to Messenia, Greece. More than 500 people were reported missing and presumed dead, making it one of the most catastrophic crossings of the Mediterranean in history.

- The sheer number of people missing and presumed dead gave this story heat.
- The heat was compounded by photos of the ship taken right before the disaster, showing how crowded the ship was.
- Yet it occurred far from U.S. shores, filled with non-white refugees from non-Western countries. The deceased became a faceless crowd, and thus the public was unable to personalize and relate to their stories.

 MEDIUM HEAT

- Tens of thousands of refugees arrived in Europe in 2023 alone, angering right-wing parties. Mediterranean migrant crossings had already preoccupied European leaders and public for years.
- However, the long-standing migration crisis likely led to severe attention fatigue, making the capsizing of the Adriana less, rather than more, likely to catch fire in the news because it came on the heels of so many similar stories.
- While migrant crossings had been prominent on the political agenda and public consciousness in Europe, its complexities made it a hard-to-understand problem, preventing the story from fitting into a clear and larger narrative.

 LOW FUEL

- This event did not attract much attention outside the news media except to draw some criticism on social media for how little news coverage the Adriana tragedy received compared to the Titan submersible story.
- Former President Obama highlighted this disparity in the weeks after the Adriana capsized when speaking at the Stavros Niarchos Foundation conference in Athens and then later in an interview with CNN's Christiane Amanpour.
- Otherwise, the event received very little attention from U.S. politicians or the public.

 MED. LOW OXYGEN

OUTCOMES RELATED TO THE TITAN SUBMERSIBLE MEDIA STORM:

compliance concerns, prompting calls for reform. As of July 2025, no regulatory action had been taken, but this may change as a result of the newly-released Coast Guard's findings and recommendations.
- **Lawsuit:** The family of one of the passengers, Paul-Henri Nargeolet, filed a $50 million lawsuit against OceanGate in August 2024, which is still pending.
- **OceanGate:** On July 6, 2023, OceanGate announced it had suspended all operations. As of July 2025, it was still non-operational.

Figure 5 (cont.)

conditions for an event (by which we mean a single event, a string of events, a discovery of new information about old events, etc.) to result in a media storm.

We use fire as an analogy. In the case of real fires, the "fire triangle," championed in the US by Smokey Bear, is a simple model designed to help the average person understand the conditions needed to create most fires (Bear 2019). Borrowing this fire triangle imagery, we offer a model of the three necessary conditions for media storms to occur.

- The "heat" in our model is the spark that sets off the media storm, namely an event or the discovery of information that is dramatic and often tragic. Every event is a spark, of course, but media storms spring from sparks that are especially hot. The factors that go into what makes something "hot" is, put plainly, the perceived newsworthiness of the event: the population affected, the unexpectedness (or "shock value") of the occurrence, and so on, as well as the availability of evidence (like video, photo, or audio).
- The "fuel" is the current and historical state of the political and cultural landscape against which the event occurs that might increase the salience and/or cognitive accessibility of that event. For wildfires, we can think of fuel as the amount and type (e.g., dry/wet) of flammable wood and brush in a forest. In the case of media storms, the fuel is the recent or current state of any public discussions that would increase the resonance of a given event. More specifically, the fuel in our model can take one or both of two forms: first, an existing societal awareness of the underlying issue left over from previous media coverage and, second, active debates in other policy areas or in the cultural zeitgeist that allow news outlets to *frame* the event in question in a way that will resonate against the current landscape.
- The "oxygen" is the available attention space in the news media in the first place (i.e., whether the current media agenda is already at capacity with other big stories), as well as attention the event receives beyond traditional news outlets, such as by activist groups, politicians, and/or people on social media.

Figure 1 offers a representation of the model, our homage to Smokey Bear. This figure summarizes the parts of each element and provides a visual reminder of the interconnected nature of the elements. Akin to Kingdon's (2010) policy streams model, all three elements are required for a window of opportunity – in this case, a media storm – to occur. Also as with Kingdon's model, the three elements of the fire triangle model are complex and interdependent. As one element rises, the other elements tend to rise as well. The more sensational an event (heat), for example, the more likely it is to draw attention on social media (oxygen). And the more an event taps into issues already on the political and public radar (fuel), the greater its newsworthiness (heat) will generally be. Thus, although in theory we could imagine a trade-off relationship between these elements, such that a media storm could erupt with only "Medium" levels of one element as long as the other elements were "Very High," in practice the three elements tend to all be fairly high or all be fairly low. And just as with real fires, the levels of the elements determine not only *whether* a media storm erupts but also *how big it is* and *how long it lasts*.

Are these three conditions of heat, fuel, and oxygen *jointly sufficient* to produce a media storm? That is, if an event has strong levels of all three, will a media storm definitely result? It's hard to say. In our research, we have not found any instances of an event that has strong levels of all three elements (again, at least "High" according to our categorization) but did *not* catch fire in the news. We present our fire triangle model of heat, fuel, and oxygen as the minimum conditions to prompt a media storm. If pressed, however, we would argue that strong levels of all three elements are jointly sufficient to prompt a media storm, at least in the case of US national news coverage.

Still, we can imagine scenarios where, by pure luck, even high levels of all three elements do not result in a full-blown media storm. Indeed, many of the media storms we have examined came very close to not catching fire in the national news. For example, on February 26, 2012 in Sanford, FL, Trayvon Martin – a Black seventeen-year-old boy – was walking home from the local 7-Eleven, with an iced tea and Skittles candy in his pocket, when George Zimmerman (a neighbor member of the local community watch) shot and killed him. Ultimately, the story became a media storm, but not immediately. As *New York Times* reporter Brian Stelter writes:

> "It was not until mid-March, after word spread on Facebook and Twitter, that the shooting of Trayvon by George Zimmerman, 28, was widely reported by the national news media, highlighting the complex ways that news does and does not travel in the Internet age.
>
> "That Trayvon's name is known at all is a testament to his family, which hired a tenacious lawyer to pursue legal action and to persuade sympathetic members of the news media to cover the case. Just as important, family members were willing to answer the same painful questions over and over at news conferences and in TV interviews." (Stelter 2012)

As another example, if President Obama had not declared the Flint, MI water crisis a national emergency in January 2016 (an action that definitely did not go without saying, since the crisis had been ongoing for nearly two years at that point), it is likely the media storm would not have erupted even though elements of heat, fuel, and oxygen were all already present to some degree. See Figure 6 for a chronicling of the Flint water crisis media storm.

Flint, Michigan Water Crisis Timeline
with notations of key elements of: **Heat, Fuel, & Oxygen**

Historical Context

The Flint water crisis highlighted a longstanding issue in U.S. infrastructure that had been on the public's radar for decades: lead pipes. Outlawed in new construction in 1986, existing lead pipes remained in use. Despite reports and studies on their dangers, including Obama's 2011 Reduction of Lead in Drinking Water Act and a 2012 CDC study, the issue gained little traction until the Flint crisis created a compelling narrative in 2016, years after the problem began.

2011–2013: Financial emergency

(Local) Mar 2011: The Michigan state government declares Flint in a financial emergency amidst a $25 million budget deficit.

April 2014: Water source switch and water quality issues begin

- *Apr 25, 2014:* Flint switches its water source from Lake Huron, which supplies Detroit, to the untapped Flint River to save money.
- *(Local)* Residents begin complaining of foul-smelling, discolored water and sharing images of discolored water on social media, raising initial awareness.
- Local news outlets *Detroit Free Press* and *The Flint Journal* cover increasingly urgent resident complaints.

August–October 2014: Water quality issues rise

- *Aug 2014:* City-wide tests detect *E. coli* bacteria in Flint's water, prompting boil-water advisories. City responds by dumping large amounts of disinfectant into water.
- *(Corporate) Oct 2014:* General Motors stops using Flint water because the high chloride content (resulting from the disinfectant) is corroding engine parts.
- Local news outlets (*Detroit Free Press*, *The Flint Journal*, WEYI) continue to cover citizen concerns and issues.

January–July 2015: Water issues and concerns rise amid dismissive DEQ responses

- *Sept 2015:* New concerns arise; lead contamination is confirmed by researchers, and local pediatrician finds elevated levels in children.
- *Sept 15, 2015:* Virginia Tech Professor Marc Edwards holds a press conference, revealing that one in six homes in Flint has lead water levels exceeding the EPA's legal safety threshold, with higher lead levels concentrated in the poorest neighborhoods.
- *Sept 24, 2015:* Dr. Mona Hanna-Attisha, a local Flint pediatrician who took the initiative to study lead levels before and after the water source change, confirms elevated blood lead levels in Flint's children in a press conference.
- *Celebrity Awareness:* Filmmaker Michael Moore, a Flint native, criticizes Michigan officials and begins speaking out about the crisis.

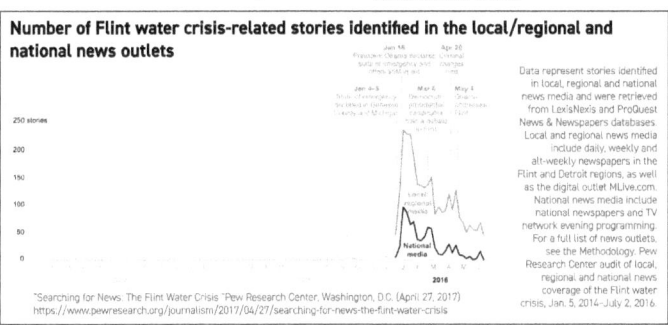

Figure 6 Timeline of media storm surrounding Flint, MI water crisis.

Flint, Michigan Water Crisis Timeline

with notations of key elements of: **Heat, Fuel, & Oxygen**

October–December 2015: Water source reverted, state of emergency declared, and social media outcries begin

- Press coverage remains mostly local, but some stories begin to be picked up in the national media; *The New York Times* prints its first stories about lead levels in Flint water in Oct 2015.
- *Oct 8, 2015:* Governor Snyder announces that Flint will switch back to Detroit's water system on the 16th, but the water remains unsafe, as the pipes continue to leach lead because of the disinfectants previously used.
- (Local) *Dec 14, 2015:* Flint Mayor declares a state of emergency.

2016: Federal interventions, celebrity attention, and national media storm

- *Jan 5th, 2016:* Governor Snyder and the state of Michigan declare a state of emergency.
- *Jan 16th, 2016:* President Obama declares a federal emergency, authorizing FEMA resources to provide clean water, filters, and other aid.
- *Jan 2016:* **Media storm ignites.**
- *Feb 28, 2016:* Star-studded #JusticeForFlint Benefit held in Flint.
- *Mar 14, 2016:* Eight-year-old Flint resident Mari Copeny writes a letter to President Obama requesting a meeting to discuss Flint's water crisis.
- *Mar 17, 2016:* Governor Snyder testifies before Congress.
- By *March 2016*, 12 lawsuits had been filed in Michigan courts.
- *May 4, 2016:* President Obama visits Flint and drinks filtered Flint water as a symbolic gesture, but residents remain skeptical of the water's safety.
- *May 2016:* Celebrity reactions include statements from Eminem and Niki Minaj, to Madonna and Pearl Jam making donations.
- *Jun 2016:* Legal charges ramp up.
- *Nov 10, 2016:* Federal judge rules against the City of Flint.

2017–2025: Settlement, more community aid, and payments

- *Mar 28, 2017:* A federal judge approves a settlement requiring Michigan to allocate $97 million to replace water lines and offer free bottled water and filters.
- *Aug 12, 2017:* Singer Bruno Mars donates $1 million to aid Flint residents.
- *Mar 2018 & 2019:* Celebrities like Jaden and Will Smith help fund bottled water and filtration systems for Flint schools.
- *Nov 2021:* Federal judge approves $626 million settlement, primarily benefiting children affected by lead poisoning.
- *Mar 2023:* Settlement and restitution payments start being distributed to Flint residents.
- *July 1, 2025:* Flint completes replacing nearly 11,000 lead pipes and restoring over 28,000 affected properties, completing the requirements of a court-ordered settlement.

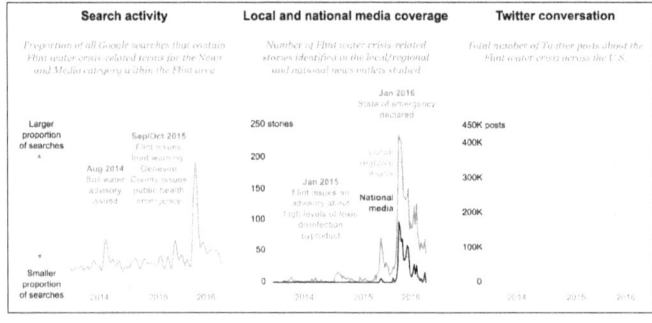

Figure 6 (cont.)

The main takeaway point from our model is that media storms are not easily predictable; the occurrence of a profoundly important event is not alone sufficient. And as with real fires, media storms can prove harmful to the people or groups in the path of the flames (e.g., to police departments during the Black Lives Matter protests) but can also, at least sometimes, prove beneficial in the long run by clearing pent-up old brush from years of neglect, making way for new growth.

Of course, our model is not perfect. We present it with at least four cautionary notes. First, the three elements of the model are interdependent (just as heat, fuel, and oxygen are interdependent in the fire triangle model), such that in some instances it might be challenging to know exactly which of the three elements to use in labeling a given aspect of a news item. Second, to avoid confusion, we should not interpret the mechanisms of media storms too literally in comparison to real fires, where combustion occurs through specific physical processes and "fire occurs whenever combustible fuel in the presence of oxygen at an extremely high temperature becomes gas" (Bear 2019). Instead, we apply the fire triangle as a useful analogy to describe the dynamic and interacting features of media storms that are often hard to discern or describe. Third, while media storms are, by definition, moments where news coverage has reached a tipping point, they are not an all-or-nothing phenomenon; some storms are bigger and last longer than others. The strength of the three elements of heat, fuel, and oxygen help determine not only whether an event prompts a media storm but also the size, scope, and duration of that storm. And even when news coverage does not reach the full tipping point of a media storm, there is important variance in how much coverage non-storm items get. Some events start to build momentum in the news and come close to catching fire but then peter out before meeting the full criteria for a media storm; we refer to these near misses as "storm fronts," discussed more in Section 7. Fourth, readers will doubtless be able to think of cases where a media storm ignited without all three criteria or needed some extra ingredient that does not fit neatly in any of the three conditions of our model to push it to media storm levels.

As the statistician George Box is attributed as saying, "all models are wrong, but some are useful" (1979). We hope our fire triangle model offers a useful mental structure for thinking about media storms.

5 The Role of Political Actors in the Fire Triangle Model

We will turn to a more detailed discussion of the heat, fuel, and oxygen elements in Section 6. But first, in this section, we animate the media storm fire triangle model by talking about the many political actors – from journalists to politicians to everyday people – whose actions help drive (or hinder) the media storm process.[13] Specifically, we'll talk about journalistic gatekeeping and muckraking; attention fatigue; activism and political maneuvering; and the importance of slogans and hashtags. The individuals behind these actions are motivated by different sets of incentives, sometimes clashing and diverging from one another. For example, a politician or official may seek to tamp down coverage of a Black person killed by police, while an activist works to increase the coverage around the same event (Lawrence 2022).

We position this discussion before detailing the heat, fuel, and oxygen elements because political actors are at the core of our model and must be accounted for in evaluating the level of each element within a given case. Media storms do not simply happen; they are the result of different people in different roles with different motivations, all making decisions about whether or not (and if so, how) to engage with a potential news item. As Lawrence states, "These occasional openings in the news, moreover, illuminate the underlying factors that drive the construction of public problems in the news" (2022: 154).

Journalistic Gatekeeping and Muckraking

Arguably, the most important political actors in the media storm process are journalists, editors, and newsrooms more broadly. They serve as gatekeepers, deciding which items make it into the news and which don't – as well as how much agenda space and what type of narratives to give those items they choose to cover (Lawrence 2022). But news values are not formulaic calculations (see Section 6, Heat for more). Journalists individually make subjective decisions about what to value and, thus, what not to value. In addition to gatekeeping, journalists can also seek to influence politics through their news coverage – a practice called "muckraking" (Chalmers 1959; Maloy 2020). In both cases, journalists use their own perspective, either subconsciously or consciously, to decide which stories to cover and how to cover them.

Thus, in our fire triangle model, we can think of the heat of an event as being its generic newsworthiness. Yet we also need to understand that journalists and editors serve as a kind of fuse governing how much to *amplify* or *suppress* the inherent heat (Zai n.d.). In making these decisions, journalists and editors put more value on some people and stories than others in ways that align with journalists' interests (Kepplinger, Brosius, and Staab 1991) or simply with their world views. These journalistic decisions often heighten the structural biases

---

[13] We include "everyday people" as "political actors" because, even if they are not pursuing a political agenda, they contribute nonetheless to the political process through their political behavior, including their attention – or inattention – to policy problems.

that are embedded in news values, such as giving greater priority to White women in cases of missing people and to the perspectives of more wealthy people in general (Jacobs et al. 2021; Jacobs and Van Spanje 2023; Slakoff and Fradella 2019; van Dalen 2012). These judgments serve to validate some voices over others.

In the case of police use of deadly force, for example, news outlets have historically validated police perspectives over Black community activists, prioritizing law enforcement as information sources and quoting them more frequently (Lawrence 2022). George Floyd's murder uncovered a wide gap in perceptions of newsworthiness between White and non-White journalists. As *Washington Post* media correspondents reported in June 2020, "Like the nation itself, news organizations across the country are facing a racial reckoning, spurred by protests from their own journalists over portrayals of minority communities and the historically unequal treatment of nonwhite colleagues" (Farhi et al. 2020).

Beyond journalists' perceptions of the inherent heat of a story, they also serve to interpret and filter the oxygen and fuel elements of our fire triangle model. For example, in our model social media attention is categorized under the element of oxygen. Yet this oxygen operates in part through journalists' decisions to cover what's happening on social media in the first place, thereby allowing social media discussions to fan the flames of preexisting news coverage, leading to more coverage in a self-reinforcing cycle (Staab 1990). Journalists also lean on social media to inform them about stories as well as evolving public values and priorities (Walters 2022; Weaver and Willnat 2016). In this way, social media shapes journalists' approach to the elements of heat and fuel.

For example, Figure 4 describes the media storm following H.R. 4437, the Border Protection, Antiterrorism, and Illegal Immigration Control Act of 2005. News outlets across the country could have decided to give a large volume of coverage to this bill when it passed the House in December of 2005. Yet the media storm did not hit until nationwide protests erupted in the spring of 2006 – captured in part through widespread discussion on social media. We argue that the oxygen from these protests was a necessary element in generating the media storm, but only because of how journalists and newsrooms operate. We can imagine a different reality, one in which a piece of legislation like H.R. 4437 would be deemed an important enough event to prompt a media storm on its own.

As a counterexample, consider again the *Boston Globe* journalists who made the intentional choice to focus countless hours of investigative reporting to uncover cases of child sexual abuse by Catholic priests. These journalists did their work in the face of aggressive pushback. The same can be said for the *New York Times* journalists who pursued the sexual assault and rape allegations against Harvey Weinstein. They could have chosen at many points to let the story drop, but their dogged reporting helped prompt a media storm with wide-reaching consequences.

Attention Fatigue

In general, there is a self-reinforcing relationship between the size and momentum of a media storm and how much fuel *and* oxygen are fed back into the storm. Regarding fuel, the eruption of a media storm puts the underlying policy issue front and center in people's minds, making it more likely that related events also get news coverage, further fueling the ongoing media storm. Regarding oxygen, as a story rises in the news, it is more likely to make its way into the conversations outside of the news media (by politicians, late-night talk shows, and people on social media, as well as issue activists). In turn, as the attention outside the news media increases, it increases the media storm itself because news outlets report on people's reactions to the news: front-page articles covering partisan responses to the story, culture pieces dissecting the significance of a *Saturday Night Live* parody of the story, and so on.

Yet we expect there is a limit to the self-reinforcing nature of fuel and oxygen in propelling media storms. Why? Because humans have a difficult time sustaining attention to a single issue over an extended period. After enough coverage of the same type of event, even talked about in different ways, attention fatigue (also called issue fatigue) can set in, signaling an information overload of news about a particular subject, or overexposure of news more generally (Gurr and Metag 2022; Neuman 1990). As Gurr and Metag summarize, "Issue fatigue denotes an individual's negative state that emerges from overexposure to an issue that is covered intensively by the news media during weeks or months" (2022: 18). Attention fatigue is especially likely to occur when the subject matter is distressing, and the underlying problems are hard to solve (as in the case of George Floyd or mass school shootings) or are hard for many to connect to their everyday lives (as in the case of climate change disasters or immigrant deportations).

Attention fatigue may affect different types of news consumers differently. For example, Tewksbury, Hals, and Bibart identify two main kinds of consumers: *selectors*, who "confine the majority of their news exposure to specific topics," and *browsers*, who use "news media to obtain information on a range of topics" (2008: 257). We can imagine that in the case of selectors for whom a media storm falls within their topics of interest (e.g., a media storm involving a celebrity for a person who seeks out celebrity news), attention fatigue will take longer to set in, if it ever does. By contrast, browsers may be more susceptible to attention fatigue, especially in cases where a media storm drags on, such as with the COVID-19 global pandemic (Ford, Douglas, and Barrett 2023), when information overload could lead them to satisfice in their search for additional information and knowledge (Prabha et al. 2007). Research is needed on how news consumption styles interact with – and further drive – the dynamics of media storms.

The result of attention fatigue can be issue avoidance, where people actively avoid the news about a particular issue (e.g., the war in Ukraine, ongoing since 2014 and especially since Russia's invasion in 2021, or the Syrian refugee crisis, ongoing since 2011) (Skovsgaard and Andersen 2020). And during prolonged and sustained coverage or an overexposure where avoidance is less of an option (e.g., news coverage of the global pandemic starting in 2020), people may respond to information overload by adopting a "the news will find me" approach, especially if they have low trust in the traditional media (Goyanes, Ardèvol-Abreu, and Gil De Zúñiga 2023). This behavior can heighten people's exposure to misinformation and disinformation (Newman et al. 2021). News outlets, savvy to the ebbs and swells of audience attention, will respond to – or proactively anticipate – people's attention fatigue in a given issue area by giving *less* coverage to that issue and related events.

The shift that can occur over time from self-reinforcing media coverage to attention fatigue is nicely captured in Downs' (1972) issue-attention cycle mentioned in Section 2, where the realization of the complexities of a problem give way directly to declining interest in the problem. In our fire triangle model, the duration of a media storm hinges upon the interplay of oxygen, fuel, and heat, but not necessarily in a linear manner. At least in the case of fuel, we theorize a parabolic correlation between the continued fuel of an event and the amount and duration of news coverage the event receives: initially in an upward direction but then in a downward direction if/when attention fatigue sets in.

Activism and Political Maneuvering

Scholars measure media storms by the level of news coverage a story receives, but in many ways news coverage is an endpoint in the activism and political process. Beneath any news coverage paid to an issue – and beneath periods of time when the issue receives no news coverage – are activist groups, lobbyists, and other political actors constantly at work to promote their issues of concern, framed from their perspective, and sometimes to keep items *out* of the news.

Activism and political maneuvering around a policy issue can lay the groundwork to capitalize on the spark from an event to ignite a media storm. Activism, in this context, functions as both the fuel to be ignited and the oxygen of amplification that can help produce and sustain a media storm, and the two elements can be so entwined as to make it difficult to differentiate what constitutes fuel versus oxygen.

Activism can provide fuel for a media storm through the cumulative activity within an issue area. Prior media storms and even non-storm coverage (including storm fronts) contribute to this fuel, shaping the landscape against which new events unfold. But if the issue landscape has a robust activist environment, it can make it easier for a related event to catch fire in the news. This activist environment can span small ad hoc grassroots efforts to the strategic efforts of long-established interest groups. In 2014, for example, the protests and Black Lives Matter movement organization that followed Michael Brown's killing were populated not only by people in the local community of Ferguson, MO. Many activists and protestors traveled from around the country to help fuel the movement (Altman 2014). The 2014 organization and codification of the Black Lives Matter movement meant that when George Floyd was murdered in 2020, the movement's infrastructure was already strongly established. This preexisting network allowed mobilization to occur within hours of the video of Floyd's murder being released, with marches and rallies organized across the country (Dunivin et al. 2022). Mobilization could not have happened so quickly without those networks and structures already in place. The fuel activism can provide for a media storm that extends beyond activists themselves and into the networks that activists establish with journalists, politicians, and other political actors (Lawrence 2022; Litterer, Jurgens, and Card 2023; Montpetit and Harvey 2018). Additionally, by strategically framing an issue, activists can broaden the scope of information and lend a sense of legitimacy to the activist groups and the causes they champion. In doing so, activists provide additional fuel for potential future media storms (Houston, Pfefferbaum, and Rosenholtz 2012).

At the same time, activism can provide the oxygen for a media storm by amplifying news coverage of a related event throughout these established networks, for example by posting and engaging with followers on social media, emailing established listservs of supporters and enlisting their engagement, and lobbying politician contacts to make statements in support of the activists' aims (Brown, Block Jr, and Stout 2020; Reny and Newman 2021). For example, by the time of George Floyd's murder, the Black Lives Matter activists had already constructed networks beyond the activists themselves via an engaged audience on social media and established connections with journalists – the latter facilitated in part through an increase in resources in newsrooms available to devote to coverage of police use of deadly force (Anderson et al. 2022; Cowart, Blackstone, and Riley 2022).

These network links between activists and journalists can create a positive feedback loop of information and reaction, especially during media storms, when journalists are especially likely to reach out to activist groups for their perspectives on unfolding events (Montpetit and Harvey 2018; Ploughman 1995). The media storm also lowers the media's gatekeeping threshold in the drive for more coverage, allowing the entrance of new viewpoints (Litterer, Jurgens, and Card 2023). The collaborative efforts between activists and journalists create a fertile ground for the growth of organizations associated with the cause. This growth, in turn, facilitates increased funding and elevates the profiles of the activists involved (McAdam 2017; Montpetit and Harvey 2018). This added credibility helps meet what Lawrence (2022) describes as the "threshold of power," which reflects the influence of institutional and social power structures on media coverage. Raising the profile of activist networks lends new legitimacy and credence to their cause, and this power dynamic can enable (or in some cases force) journalists to cover events and perspectives they might have otherwise ignored.

We must also consider the actions that activists and other political actors, including crisis management teams, often take toward influencing whether an event becomes a media storm. To extend our fire analogy, activist groups may try to increase the chances of a policy issue they care about catching fire in the news by strategically adding their own heat, fuel, and/or oxygen to the situation, as was the case in the Civil Rights Movement where activists staged high-profile sit-ins and members like Rosa Parks defied local laws in order to be arrested (Mazumder 2018). Similarly, the Gay Rights Movement effectively used symbolic actions, such as same-sex couples applying for marriage licenses in states where it was illegal, to provoke legal battles and ensuing media coverage. In the lead-up to the 2015 Supreme Court decision on marriage equality (*Obergefell* v. *Hodges*), activists strategically framed these acts of civil disobedience to highlight the injustice of marriage bans, forcing the issue into the public and legal discourse. In our fire triangle model, efforts like these (whether by activists or other political actors) serve to heighten an already smoldering fire. We invite the reader to consider whether some tactics by issue activists or other political actors might be appropriately labeled "arson" in the fire triangle analogy.

However, not all groups actively seek media attention during the unfolding of events related to their cause. For instance, organizations like the National Rifle Association (NRA) may strategically avoid media coverage to prevent the escalation of a media storm that could be detrimental to their goals. These groups may even implement obstacles to dampen potential media attention and control the narrative surrounding specific events, such as school shootings (Gammon 2018). In the world of crisis management, often the strongest strategy in the wake of a scandal involving a political figure or a company is to issue a denial, even in the face of strong evidence of wrongdoing (Huang 2006). Another strategy employed by politicians as well as interest groups is to "wag the dog" by offering to the media another juicy item far afield from the news item of concern. Applying the fire triangle analogy, we can think of these actions as fire prevention or containment measures, akin to clear cutting or trench digging in a given issue area or muffling flames with a blanket or water once a fire breaks out.

Whatever the form of the activity surrounding a specific event, activism and other political maneuvering can have long-reaching effects by changing the very landscape of an issue area. For example, just as the removal of vegetation in a forest sets the stage for rapid regeneration of highly flammable conditions, political interventions can create even more combustible environments.

Slogans and Hashtags

For activists and all other political actors, strategic messaging is important for both amplifying problems of concern (oxygen) and laying the groundwork to make these problems and perspectives readily accessible going forward (fuel). Slogans have always been a powerful tool in the strategic messaging toolbox (Van De Velde 2022). For example, the 1960s youth protest movement includes pithy slogans like "My Generation," and more action-oriented ones like Timothy Leary's "Turn on, tune in, drop out," which were successful in pulling together people toward common goals (Kent 2001). In the changing media landscape, messaging strategies have evolved from letters to the editor or phone calls to a local TV news station to become more nationalized and more visual. Social media platforms in particular have become the new arena for activists and issue publics (i.e., people who care strongly about single issues like abortion or gun control) to fight for relevancy about a cause and to compete for attention from the media and the public (Johann 2022; Mortensen and Neumayer 2021).

In this arena, slogans in the form of hashtags have become the coin of the realm, allowing communities to build around them online (Peters and Allan 2022). Hashtags serve as both fuel and oxygen, providing a throughline for discussions of related events, past and present, and making it easier to amplify those events when they happen.

Hashtags are powerful not only for fostering and sustaining media storms but also for "exploiting" a crisis event that has prompted a media storm. For example, Hunt (2022) examines the competing ways in which proabortion and antiabortion activists used social media, including hashtags, to capitalize on the COVID-19 pandemic (e.g., #SheMakesHerSafeChoice versus #AbortionIsNotEssential). Through social media, the two sides exhibited "movement-countermovement" dynamics in their competition to frame abortion against the context of the ongoing pandemic (Hunt 2022).

Memes can serve a similar function to hashtags, providing culturally relevant visual information that creates a sense of community using irony or playfulness to impart a message (McVicker 2021). If the meme connects with enough people online, that group then becomes a new audience giving attention to an item, breathing oxygen into a potential or ongoing media storm. Hashtags and memes are easily accessible for average people to use and create on social media, broadening the scope of potential fuel and oxygen for media storms in the modern era.

Consider, for example, the success of the #MeToo hashtag posted by celebrity Alyssa Milano on Twitter on October 15, 2017. This hashtag went viral in the wake of two in-depth investigative pieces about Harvey Weinstein written by the *New York Times* on October 5 and *The New Yorker* on October 10. Those stories made huge waves, erupting into a media storm, with the #MeToo hashtag going viral on social media. This social media oxygen in turn helped amplify the story and helped create the environment that took down several powerful men perpetuating the offenses. However, the hashtag of #MeToo was born nearly eleven years earlier on MySpace (an early social media platform) by survivor and activist Tarana Burke in 2006. Burke's efforts, though impactful in grassroots advocacy aimed at marginalized communities, did not catch fire in the mainstream media. The hashtag lay relatively dormant until it was picked up by Milano, whose celebrity status added heat along with the oxygen of her social media post. This discrepancy in impact can be attributed in part to structural inequalities within media and public attention: Burke, as a Black woman and noncelebrity, did not have access to the same platform or perceived status needed to amplify the message to mainstream audiences. Conversely, Milano was able to leverage her celebrity to push the hashtag into the public consciousness. The hashtag, in turn, gave the media storm more oxygen (and sustained fuel). This case illustrates how racial and social hierarchies often shape which voices and narratives gain traction in broader movements, despite the foundational work of activists like Burke (Garcia 2017).

6 Necessary Elements of Media Storms: Heat, Fuel, and Oxygen

In this section, we describe the three elements of our model in more detail. For each, we map the concept of the element onto multiple case studies, including our running example of police use of deadly force. For this thread of our discussion, we refer the reader to Figure 7, which shows the rise and fall of news coverage about police use of force based on an original quantitative dataset we compiled from *New York Times* and *Wall Street Journal* coverage, 2010–22 (5,791 articles in total). Additionally, in our discussion for each element (heat, fuel, oxygen), we showcase two examples of news items that became media storms, each paralleled with a similar news item that did not, where the largest difference was the element in question. For the first example in each section, we compare two news items surrounding individual people (e.g., Britney Spears versus Amanda Bynes). For the second example, we compare two news items surrounding larger policy problems or issues (e.g., children's deaths by guns versus children's deaths in auto accidents). In doing so, we hope to highlight how media storms can occur in the case of both episodic and thematic news coverage (Iyengar 1991).

Recall our argument that in order to become a media storm, a news item needs to satisfy all three conditions of heat, fuel, and oxygen at a high level. The three elements tend to reinforce one another, as our examples make clear. We furthermore posit that if all three conditions are met at high levels, a media storm will erupt. When it does, a media storm can be enough to change the public debate, the way we communicate about an issue, and sometimes even policy (see Section 7).

Heat

In the case of real fires, "a heat source is responsible for the initial ignition of fire, and is also needed to maintain the fire and enable it to spread. Heat allows fire to spread by drying out and preheating nearby fuel and warming surrounding air" (Bear 2019). In our media storm model, the heat is the perceived newsworthiness of the event or newly revealed information responsible for catching the media's attention. In many cases, the kind of news item that prompts a media storm is a "focusing event," defined as "an event that is sudden; relatively uncommon; can be reasonably defined as harmful or revealing the possibility of potentially greater future harms; has harms that are concentrated in a particular geographical area or community of interest; and that is known to policy makers and the public simultaneously" (Birkland 1998). A natural disaster like Hurricane Katrina in 2005, for example, or a shocking event like the January 6, 2021, attack on the US

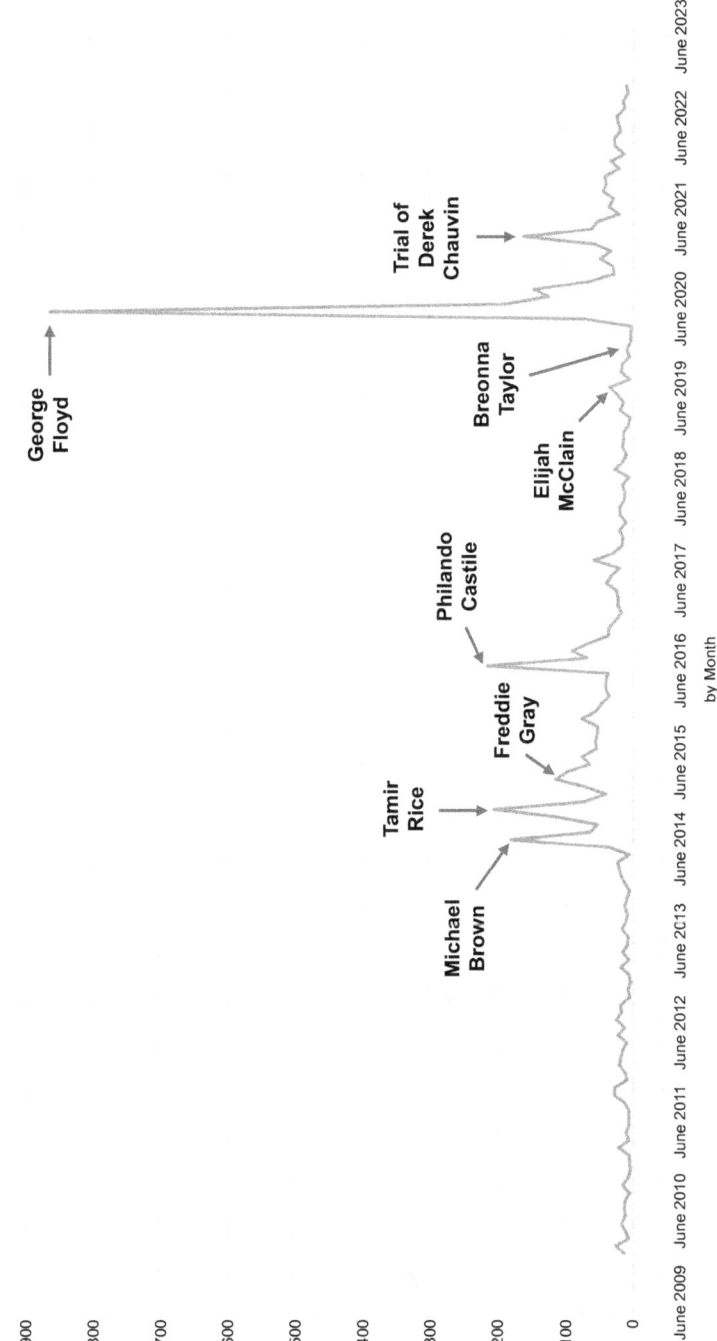

Figure 7 Levels of US news coverage about police use of force, by month, 2010–22.

Capitol Building can serve as a sudden and large match strike that initiates a media storm. But other news items can also prompt media storms, such as a planned event (e.g., an election, or an international summit) or a long-simmering policy problem (e.g., the Flint water crisis described more in the section "Oxygen" and featured in Figure 6). In the Flint case, the event itself (a water crisis resulting in lead poisoning of children) was certainly "hot" but not the kind of sudden focusing event Birkland and other scholars have pointed to as being a usual suspect for prompting a surge of media attention.

The more newsworthy the event, the hotter it is. Newsworthiness is generally defined by how surprising and sensational a news item is, how large a population of people it affects, the nature of the people involved (e.g., children, celebrities), its relevance for a given readership/viewership, and so on (Gans 2004). In 2015, for example, wildfires in Indonesia resulted in 6.4 million acres of land burned and the cause of nearly 100,000 deaths in Indonesia, Malaysia, and Singapore (World Bank Report 2016). Yet those wildfires did not receive nearly as much US news coverage as the 2019–20 wildfires in Australia even though the Australian wildfires resulted in fifty-nine million acres but far fewer deaths (thirty-three) (Clarke et al. 2022). A likely explanation for this discrepancy in coverage is that American readers feel more kinship to Australia than to Indonesia (Rouf and Wainwright 2020). And the Australian wildfires in turn received less US news coverage than the 2019 wildfires in California, where 259,823 acres burned and three people died (Cagle 2019).

Importantly, as discussed in Section 5, Journalistic Gatekeeping and Muckraking, the heat of an event is not strictly predetermined by the features of a given event but rather interpreted and amplified by journalists in deciding which events to cover and how to cover them. With the role of journalistic gatekeepers in mind, many scholars have offered overlapping lists of news values. For example, Harcup and O'Neill (2001, 2017) build on canonical work by scholars including Galtung and Ruge (1965) to present a list of news values that determine a story's perceived newsworthiness (see Sidebar). Note that item 9 connects with the concept of "fuel" in our fire triangle model.

SIDEBAR: NEWS VALUES AS PRESENTED IN HARCUP AND O'NEIL (2017: 1471)

1. *The power elite*: Stories concerning powerful individuals, organisations or institutions.
2. *Celebrity:* Stories concerning people who are already famous.

(cont.)

3. *Entertainment:* Stories concerning sex, showbusiness, human interest, animals, an unfolding drama, or offering opportunities for humorous treatment, entertaining photographs or witty headlines.
4. *Surprise:* Stories that have an element of surprise and/or contrast.
5. *Bad news:* Stories with particularly negative overtones, such as conflict or tragedy.
6. *Good news:* Stories with particularly positive overtones, such as rescues and cures.
7. *Magnitude:* Stories that are perceived as sufficiently significant either in the numbers of people involved or in potential impact.
8. *Relevance:* Stories about issues, groups and nations perceived to be relevant to the audience.
9. *Follow-up:* Stories about subjects already in the news.
10. *Newspaper agenda:* Stories that set or fit the news organisation's own agenda.

In general, we expect that the news values that determine the newsworthiness of a story translate proportionally to the heat of an item in our media storm model. For instance, if a story involving a celebrity is significantly more newsworthy than the same story not involving a celebrity, then it should be significantly hotter in terms of its potential to prompt a media storm. However, this notion deserves to be tested. It's possible, for example, that the ratio of "bad news" to "good news" produced by general news values principles is different in the context of media storms. Although we can think of a few cases of media storms centered on positive stories (e.g., the United Nations' adoption of the Kyoto Protocol in 1997 to reduce greenhouse gases, Captain Sully's rescue of Flight 1549 in 2009, or the Chilean miners' rescue in 2010), even these items involve potential tragedy at their core. To our great disappointment, the news coverage surrounding pygmy hippopotamus Moo Deng in 2024 (amplified by internet memes and a *Saturday Night Live* sketch by Bowen Yang that every human should experience) met our empirical criteria for a *storm front* but not a media storm. It's possible that there are disproportionately fewer media storm equivalents of the purely feel-good articles that round out day-to-day news, although that might change over time and/or when considering media storms in different contexts (e.g., on social media versus traditional media). (See Soroka and Krupnikov 2021's excellent work, appropriately titled *The Increasing Viability of Good News*.)

One key factor of perceived newsworthiness, of course, is whether the event can be depicted not only in words but also in images. Consider, for example, the media storm that followed the 1955 death of Emmett Till, a Black fourteen-year-old-boy. A White woman had accused Till of offending her in a grocery store and, days later, her husband and another man abducted Till, beat him, shot him in the head, and sank his body in a river. After Till's body was recovered, his mother, Mamie Till, insisted on an open-casket funeral so that people could see her son's bloated and mutilated face. Although only Black magazines and newspapers like *Jet* and the *Chicago Defender* printed the photos of Till's corpse, the very existence of photographic evidence capturing the brutality of Till's lynching helped ignite a media storm across news outlets in the US and around the world (Goldsby 1996). The media storm had an effect, increasing White people's awareness of violence against Black men and boys, especially in the Jim Crow South (Goldsby 1996). Had Mamie Till not insisted on making the visual evidence of her son's lynching available to the public, Emmett Till's story likely would not be imprinted on American history. This case also illustrates the power of activism in pulling the attention of the media toward an issue, long neglected or otherwise.

The more photo/audio/video evidence there is of an event, the hotter it is. The BP oil spill in 2010 likely prompted such a strong media storm because of the graphic photo evidence not only of the spill itself but also of the oil-coated pelicans, whales, and other wildlife (often dead as a result of the spill). And as with real fire, the more follow-up events or information that unfurl from the initial spark, the more likely the media storm is to grow, and the longer it will likely last. For example, the Syrian migration crisis during 2015–16 generated a series of media storms that kept building upon themselves because of devastating imagery of migrants killed at sea, including a searing photo of the drowned body of the two-year-old Syrian toddler Aylan Kurdi. These images applied even greater heat, keeping the migration crisis in the news (Douai, Bastug, and Akca 2022; Moyles 2017).

Thus, the duration of an event's heat (akin to the length of a match) also matters. The more additional newsworthy items that unfold over the course of a media storm, intensifying the original heat and extending the event's urgency and tangibility, the larger and longer the media storm will be. However, these larger and longer media storms will eventually hit attention fatigue. The Syrian migration crisis, for example, did not end after 2016, but the media and the public moved on to a new story, likely in part because the imagery was so distressing.

Thinking about our motivating case of police use of deadly force, the element of heat helps explain why some events have had an easier time catching fire in the news than others. Rodney King's beating in 1991 and George Floyd's murder in 2020 were both captured on film – and if they had not been, there's a good chance the general public would never have known about either (Lee 2020). When police shot and killed Tamir Rice in Cleveland, OH in 2014, a key fact that differentiated his death from that of so many other unarmed Black people was that he was only twelve years old. (Again, Figure 7 shows a timeline of news coverage of police use of deadly force.) And when police shot and killed Philando Castile in his car during a traffic stop in Falcon Heights, MN in 2016, the story was more newsworthy than others both because Castile's girlfriend, Diamond Reynolds, and her four-year-old daughter were in the car with him when he was killed and because Reynolds posted a livestream video on Facebook from within the car shortly after Castile was shot. Images and videos from prior incidents laid a foundation of awareness and empathy, building a base for future stories to resonate. Each subsequent event compounded the shock through additional graphic visuals, amplifying public attention and emotional impact. Activists who had organized in the wake of previous incidences of violence were ready to push out the story and imagery to their networks to further stoke outrage and activism.

In short, the likelihood that a story will catch fire in the news is shaped first and foremost by how newsworthy the nature of the story is both in the facts surrounding the story (as interpreted and curated by journalists) and in whether photo/audio/video evidence exists, helping to make the story more engaging to an audience.

We turn now to our first qualitative examples of media storm versus non-storm items. We do not mean to suggest that the two items in each example pair (media storm versus non-storm) are identical. Rather, our aim here is to draw illustrative parallels between similar events, one of which sparked a media storm and one of which did not, as a way of putting our theoretical model into the motion of real events and showcasing the importance of each element of the fire triangle model.

Heat Example 1: Britney Spears versus Amanda Bynes

Britney Spears, a raging pop phenomenon and the highest-earning female musician from the years 2001 to 2012, began exhibiting mental health challenges starting in 2006. She shaved her head, lost her temper with paparazzi, and was photographed driving with her infant son on her lap using one hand to hold him and the other hand to drive. After her highly publicized divorce from and custody dispute with actor and dancer Kevin Federline in 2007, she was hospitalized for a mental breakdown that was widely covered by the media. In

2008, her father petitioned for and was awarded a temporary conservatorship, giving him the right to make decisions about almost every aspect of Spears' health, money, and personal life. This temporary ruling turned into a permanent one later in 2008, leaving Spears in her father's control for thirteen years. During the first twelve years of Spears' conservatorship, the details were largely kept private or shared only by third parties (Day, Stark, and Coscarelli 2021). However, during a routine proceeding on April 27, 2021, Spears submitted a request to speak directly to the judge, and the judge scheduled Spears' testimony for June 23, 2021. During that June testimony, Spears revealed jarring details of her conservatorship, including having an intrauterine device implanted against her will to prevent her from having additional children. Her twenty-four-minute statement occurred in a public court session and was audio-streamed for the media and public, prompting intense public support for the #FreeBritney movement and igniting a media storm, with the hashtag proliferating traditional news as well as social media. On November 12, 2021, Spears' conservatorship was terminated.

Nickelodeon star and actress Amanda Bynes suffered a fate similar to Spears, but her case amassed far less media attention, no viral hashtags, and no media storm. Bynes' career flourished from 2006 to 2012, but in 2012 she began exhibiting concerning behavior, online and offline, and was arrested for DUIs, hit and runs, and reckless driving. These incidents led to her admittance into a psychiatric hospital. Two years later, in 2014, her mother became the conservator of her estate and person, with full oversight of Bynes' finances and personal life. In 2022, after nine years under her mother's conservatorship and ongoing social media posts calling attention to her case – and, notably, shortly after the termination of Spears' conservatorship – Bynes filed a petition for termination that was approved.

Both these news items center on celebrities who endured mental health struggles resulting in personal and financial conservatorships, both of whom garnered social media attention around the fact that they wanted to be released from these conservatorships. Yet Spears' case became a media storm, while Bynes' case did not. The explanation is likely that Spears was simply more famous than Bynes, and thus more newsworthy, giving her efforts to end her conservatorship more heat to catch fire in the news (Gans 2004). The heat of Spears' case was heightened by the graphic details she shared in her June 2021 testimony, with the audio evidence of her testimony and the use of the popular #FreeBritney hashtag adding even more heat.

Of course, the heat of Spears' fame was not alone sufficient to prompt a media storm. Had Spears' case (or Bynes' case) occurred decades earlier, the social context would likely not have been as hospitable to a media storm. Instead, the (relative) de-stigmatization of mental health issues by the 2020s provided a strong landscape (fuel) to catch the spark of the news item (see our comparison of Thomas Eagleton and John Fetterman in Section 6, Fuel). And Spears' case was reinforced by the widespread advocacy (oxygen) from her fans, who rallied around the #FreeBritney movement on social media in higher numbers (likely due to her higher level of fame) than Bynes secured on social media. Thus, both cases contained fuel, but Spears' case contained much more heat and, partially as a result, much more oxygen. In contrast, Bynes lower level of stardom and the lack of an explosive court testimony limited the amount of heat her case generated and, relatedly, the public support for her cause.

Heat Example 2: Children's Deaths by Guns versus Children's Deaths in Auto Accidents

Despite child deaths resulting from auto accidents being approximately equivalent to those caused by guns, the former receives considerably less media coverage. Moreover, the vast majority of news coverage about children's gun deaths centers on high-profile school shootings, such as those at Columbine, Sandy Hook, and Parkland, even though school shootings account for less than 1% of children's deaths by guns. Lawrence and Birkland (2004) explain how media attention to child gun deaths during school shootings is driven by newsworthiness – school shootings have high news value – as well as connections to popular culture and debates on gun control by activists, politicians, and journalists, creating a reinforcing cycle. In contrast to school shootings, news coverage has "virtually ignored" other forms of gun violence that kill children, like juvenile crime (Lawrence and Birkland 2004: 1196).

News coverage of children's deaths in auto accidents is, by contrast, quite scarce. These deaths lack the same shock value as school shootings, making them tragically unnewsworthy. Unlike the sudden and dramatic nature of school shootings, the gradual and cumulative nature of child deaths from auto accidents (as well as gun violence outside the context of school shootings) diminishes societal awareness and urgency (Nixon 2011). Because these kinds of tragedies, which Nixon (2011) labels "slow violence," mount gradually instead of suddenly; they have a disproportionately weak ability to catch hold in the media. These cases also suffer from a lack of a strong advocacy environment that, if present, could amplify imagery and stories via networks of supporters, helping push for news coverage.

Paradoxically, government initiatives to reduce child deaths from auto accidents are more pronounced than those aimed at gun violence. There is a lack of political will to address child gun deaths with the same urgency (Price 2022). This disparity in political response may be attributed to several factors. Some proponents of and activists for gun rights may view child gun deaths as an inevitable consequence of safeguarding Second Amendment liberties. Note, however, that in the 1980s, when seatbelts were first regulated, there was also strong pushback against requiring seatbelts, including for children (Bae et al. 2014). Additionally, a striking racial disparity exists in youth killed by gun violence, with Black and low-income youth being disproportionately affected. These demographic disparities dampen the perceived heat of the event, making it more challenging for gun violence to gain media attention (Lawrence 2022), and also contribute to a lack of cohesive policy initiatives, as Hispanic and White youth gun deaths have also risen in recent years (Keating 2022).

Fuel

Fuel, in the case of real fires, is the combustible material, "characterized by its moisture content, size, shape, quantity, and the arrangement in which it is spread over the landscape. The moisture content determines how easily it will burn" (Bear 2019). In our media storm model, the fuel is the combustible material that has piled up in topical, societal, or political proximity to the igniting event. This fuel can take one or both of two primary forms. First, a recent history of media coverage given to similar or related events can make it easier for a media storm to catch hold (although recall the important caveat of attention fatigue from Section 5). The second kind of fuel is the current backdrop of political, economic, and/or social conditions that might allow an event to be framed in terms of those salient conditions. The more relevant either source of fuel is – that is, the more that recent related media coverage is still on the nation's radar and/or the more the news item can be framed in terms of other current conditions – the stronger the fuel will be in feeding a media storm.

The *first type of fuel* – a recent history of similar media coverage – helps prompt a media storm because recent media coverage of an issue or type of event primes that issue in the public consciousness, making it easier for subsequent events to resonate with the public. In turn, this public awareness makes it easier for journalists to explain a story effectively, both because they have to offer less educational context to explain the landscape to readers/viewers and because it's simply easier for journalists to write articles about events related to stories in which they are already steeped. This first type of fuel is thus determined by journalistic and societal momentum; indeed, the best indicator of how much news coverage a policy issue receives in a given time period is how much coverage it received in the previous time period (Boydstun 2013). For instance, Litterer, Jurgens, and Card (2023) examine the multiple surges in media coverage following the trial of Derek Chauvin (convicted of murdering George

Floyd) and find that "after an event or issue has received extensive coverage at a given outlet, it is seen as more newsworthy by reporters and editors at that same outlet, who will therefore be more likely to write or publish additional coverage of it" (6347). This heightened newsworthiness creates a demand for future coverage and for related frames that appeal to a wide array of consumers.

As an example of this first type of fuel, recall the intense media coverage of Hilary Clinton's personal email server controversy while she was Secretary of State in March of 2015. After Wikileaks released her hacked emails in July and October of 2016, the media began relentless coverage that, coupled with the heat of Clinton running for president, created a self-reinforcing cycle. Each new story about the issue gained traction simply because it echoed and amplified an already pervasive narrative. This repetition also solidified the email controversy as a shorthand for broader concerns about Clinton's trust and transparency, making it easier for subsequent, "but what about her emails?," coverage to feel relevant, regardless of its substantive importance (Searles and Banda 2019).

Past coverage, in other words, creates a *throughline* – a shared social narrative – to which journalists can hook relevant subsequent news items and activists can hook advocacy messaging. Consider media coverage surrounding the Sackler family and various lawsuits filed against members of the family and their company, Purdue Pharma, over allegations that the family and company knowingly misled doctors and the public about the risks of the drug OxyContin. Although none of the surges of news coverage around this case met the empirical criteria of a media storm, there were several storm fronts (i.e., surges in news coverage that nearly became media storms). We expect that the coverage came as close to erupting into a storm as it did because of the groundwork laid by two forms of previous coverage: ongoing news coverage of the opioid crisis in the US, and the history of media storms surrounding legal efforts to hold tobacco companies responsible for knowingly misleading the public about the health consequences of smoking (e.g., the Tobacco Master Settlement Agreement in 1998 between the largest US tobacco companies and the attorneys general of forty-six states). By the time of the Sackler family scandal, however, these historical storms were old enough to not provide enough fuel for a storm to catch.

The *second type of fuel* – a way of framing a news item such that it taps into current societal conditions – helps prompt a media storm because linking a news item to current context can amplify its perceived relevance in people's minds (and, thus, in the minds of journalists). In doing so, this second type of fuel can help bring in new voices, new perspectives, and can result in new ways of framing an event to align and capture the zeitgeist of the moment. Consider the death of Supreme Court Justice Ruth Bader Ginsburg on September 18, 2020.

Her death would have drawn a rush of media coverage regardless of when it occurred. Yet coming less than two months before the 2020 US presidential election, news outlets were able to frame the event not only as the death of a historical figure but also as a political opportunity for whoever took (Biden) or kept (Trump) the White House to shape the future of the Supreme Court. Ginsburg's death tied into the narrative of uncertainty amid the 2020 presidential election.[14] Or consider the tragic case of a ten-year-old rape survivor in Ohio who, in 2022 following the Supreme Court's *Dobbs* decision overturning *Roe v. Wade*, had to travel to Indiana to get an abortion. This child's challenge in getting abortion access almost certainly would not have become national news if did not provide a flashpoint case study for the current national debate on abortion policy (Folkenflik 2022). Also at play here were the robust activist networks around the issue of abortion, who elevated her case to catch news outlets' attention.

In our media storm model, the first type of fuel is almost never fully consumed, since media attention almost always moves on to the next hot event before the previous event/problem is fully addressed and resolved. Readers are invited to come up with even a single example where news coverage stayed locked on the object of a media storm until an underlying policy problem was truly solved. This tendency to move on before an issue is resolved is partly due to the attention fatigue we have already discussed, whereby prolonged focus on a particular issue or event leads over time to declining public and, thus, media interest (either in response to or in anticipation of waning public interest, or through news outlets lurching to the next hot story). It is also easy for items in the news, including media storms involving salacious scandals, to be overshadowed by the next hot story (Nyhan 2015). Thus, each storm leaves behind some amount of unconsumed fuel in the form of unresolved, but still salient policy questions, made even more dry and consumable from the previous fire of attention. This fuel can then be taken up by groups and activists looking to draw media attention to the next gripping event when it comes back around.

As for the second type of fuel, current conditions, be they economic or political or cultural or something else, serve as a kind of kindling to news items that can be framed in related ways, inviting the fire in that direction. Thus, for most underlying policy problems most of the time, there's always the potential of both types of fuel. The question in both cases – the dried fuel from previous media events and the kindling of current conditions that could be

---

[14] Though this narrative was partially dampened when Justice Amy Coney Barrett was quickly confirmed to replace Ginsburg on October 27, 2020, days before the 2020 general election.

linked to the news item at hand – is how *much* fuel is available, and how dry (i.e., salient and pressing) it is.

Thinking again about our motivating case of police use of deadly force, the fact that George Floyd's horrific murder in 2020 was captured on video played a major role (heat) in sparking the media storm that followed. Yet this media storm was also fueled by the underlying context of previous well-known cases of police (and citizen) violence against unarmed Black men. The movement to dignify the worth of Black lives is multifaceted, "the collective labor of a wide range of Black liberation organizations each which [*sic*] their own distinct histories" (Roberts 2018). But by 2020, this movement had been summarized and made immediately accessible (and shareable online) by the hashtag and accompanying catch phrase #BlackLivesMatter.

Many White Americans might think that the hashtag #BlackLivesMatter developed around the time of Michael Brown's death, in Ferguson MO, in November 2014. That was the first time the hashtag made a sizeable blip on Twitter. But it was created more than a year earlier, in July 2013, when George Zimmerman was acquitted of Trayvon Martin's murder. People reacted to the news of the acquittal on Twitter, including the first use of the #BlackLivesMatter hashtag by the two Black women activists, Alicia Garza and Patrisse Cullor (Day 2015). Though the hashtag was used in subsequent cases of police use of deadly force against Black people, it was mainly confined to certain corners of Twitter (Clayton 2018). However, it created fuel that would be available for future events and future activists to operationalize. Thus, the media storm following Floyd's murder was fueled by the first type of fuel: a throughline of tragic events linking Floyd's death in 2020 with Brown's death in 2014 ... with Trayvon Martin's death in 2012 ... all the way back to Rodney King's beating in 1991 (Lawrence 2022), Emmett Till's lynching in 1955, and beyond. This case, as with the MeToo example (where the #MeToo hashtag was born years before it caught hold), helps highlight the particular ability that hashtags and catch phrases have to simplify complex concepts, making them easier for people (and the news media) to register and keep top of mind (Van De Velde 2022).

The media storm following Floyd's murder was also fueled by the second type of fuel, in that it occurred in 2020, shortly after the COVID-19 global pandemic began. The combined health and economic stresses – both of which disproportionately affected Black and brown Americans (Bambra, Lynch, and Smith 2021; White 2021) – produced fuel in the form of a tinderbox of frustrations (Laurencin and Walker 2020; ABC News 2020), heightening the public protests (Arora 2020) and making it even easier for activists to leverage and news outlets and the public to latch onto the story about Floyd's murder and the broader concept of a racial reckoning. National Public Radio (NPR) reporter

Scott Horsley used this exact term, "tinderbox," when covering the story on June 1, 2020 (Horsley 2020):

> The death of a black man at the hands of a white police officer has sparked days of civil unrest in the United States. Those sparks have landed in a tinderbox assembled over decades of economic inequality, now made worse by the coronavirus pandemic. (Scott Horsley)

NPR reporter Noel King further captured the notion of this tinderbox when interviewing a man participating in a BLM protest in the summer of 2020 (Inskeep and King 2020):

> NOEL KING: I met a man who was there with his wife, his daughter and a grandbaby. His name is Miguel De Leon (ph). And he said to me, I am not an activist. My wife dragged me here. He was contemplating what was going on. And he landed on something that I've heard more than once. He said George Floyd's killing was a kind of strike three.
> MIGUEL DE LEON: We got the momentum. We're in the middle of a pandemic, economic despair. You know injustice is not going to settle right with people. They got a lot of pent-up emotion, a lot of frustration, uncertainty. So it creates an energy. So when you get a release – and it's like, that's it. Everybody coming out. They're reacting. (Steve Inskeep & Noel King)

In this way, the fuel of past media coverage to related events and the fuel of current events with relevant frameworks both helped propel the media storm following Floyd's murder. Floyd's murder also highlights how media storms can be further enflamed by the fuel of previous events that went all but unnoticed by the media and the public but that are *retroactively* brought to larger awareness in the context of a media storm, serving to prolong the media storm at hand. For example, consider three events that did *not* become media storms on their own, but later surged onto the media and public agenda during the media storm following George Floyd's death on May 25, 2020, thereby making that media storm even bigger.

- The first was Elijah McClain's encounter with police on August 24, 2019, in Aurora, CO. In an eerie parallel with Trayvon Martin's death in 2012, McClain was walking home from a convenience store when a civilian called the police to report someone looking "sketchy." Three responding officers restrained McClain on the ground, putting him in a chokehold. When paramedics arrived, they administered an excess dosage of ketamine. McClain went into cardiac arrest, dying six days later when he was removed from life support after being declared brain dead. McClain's case received

local news coverage but hardly any other attention, and no charges were filed against the officers at the time. In the wake of Floyd's death, however, national media picked up McClain's story. An online petition signed by more than 800,000 people prompted the CO District Attorney to reopen the case, leading to charges against all three officers and a homicide conviction for one.
- The following spring, on February 23, 2020, three White men in Glynn County, GA, saw Ahmaud Arbery jogging in their neighborhood. They chased him in their trucks, cornered him, and two of the men shot and killed him (the third captured the event on video that was later made public). Although the perpetrators were not police, the timing was close enough to provide retroactive fuel for the George Floyd media storm. As with Elijah McClain, Arbery's story did not make many headlines until after Floyd's death. Here too, the men in Arbery's case were not arrested until months later, following not only the George Floyd media storm but also tireless efforts by Arbery's family – led by his mother – to convince the local authorities to take action (Guardian 2020). All three men were tried and found guilty in a federal court and sentenced to prison. It stands to reason that both the media storm following Floyd's death and the amplification advocacy of Arbery's mother, Wanda Cooper-Jones, played essential roles. Her efforts exemplify Hooker's (2023) documentation of the disproportionate burden that Black families face, torn between the desire to seek justice and the right to "sit with loss".
- The last event we mark before George Floyd's death is the death of Breonna Taylor, who police shot and killed on March 13, 2020, during a late-night, no-knock raid on her apartment – a raid intended to interrupt drug operations by Taylor's ex-boyfriend. One of the officers was later convicted of violating Taylor's civil rights. Here too, Taylor's story did not become headline news until after Floyd's murder, at which point it helped fuel the ongoing media storm.

Combined, these events point to the importance of fuel not only as a necessary criterion for a media storm to occur but also as a key factor that helps determine how big the media storm becomes and how long it lasts. They also highlight the fact that there are many people deeply involved in nearly every item that becomes a media storm – activists, family members, and ordinary people – who keep the flames alive when attention dies down and stand ready to capitalize on future opportunities to draw attention back again.

Of course, fuel by itself is not sufficient; there is little appetite for news that is just more of the same. The heat provides the novelty of new information, whereas the fuel provides the familiar context for that new information to be more relevant. This interplay between heat and fuel ties into broader notions of communication innovation. In the world of collaborative communication technology (e.g., social media), those products that are most likely to catch hold are those that have a familiar goal or product, but with a novel process or application (Hill 2013). In this way, activists and organizers can apply familiar narratives (fuel) to novel applications (high-heat events) in order to amplify attention to their cause across and beyond their networks.

Fuel Example 1: Thomas Eagleton Depression (1972) versus John Fetterman Depression (2023)

In July 1972, the Democratic convention in Miami faced uncertainties as George McGovern, an insurgent candidate, sought a running mate against incumbent President Nixon. Despite assumptions that Ted Kennedy would join, he declined. Under time pressure, McGovern turned to Thomas Eagleton, an up-and-coming Senator from Missouri. Eagleton's Catholic background and antiabortion stance appealed to address McGovern's challenges with key voter demographics. However, within two weeks, information emerged about Eagleton's past hospitalizations and treatment (including electroshock therapy) for depression. This information erupted into a scandal and media storm that was decidedly negative, focused on concerns about Eagleton's fitness for office. On July 25, 1972, Eagleton admitted to his past treatment for depression. Despite initial defiance on the part of McGovern and Eagleton, Eagleton withdrew his VP candidacy on August 1, 1972, making his tenure as the vice president nominee just eighteen days long. Some observers say this event contributed to McGovern's defeat by Nixon. Despite the controversy, Eagleton went on to have a successful Senate career until stepping down in 1987.

Fast forward five decades to 2022, when John Fetterman (Lieutenant Governor of Pennsylvania) was campaigning for an open US Senate seat while battling clinical depression outside the public eye. In May 2022, in the midst of his heated campaign for Senate, Fetterman suffered a stroke. He went on to win the Senate race that November, but the resulting impact on his physical health worsened his depression. On February 16, 2023, he checked himself into Walter Reed Hospital after he began having thoughts of self-harm. Fetterman remained hospitalized for about two months while he underwent treatment for depression, and he was discharged from Walter Reed on March 31, 2023. After information about his treatment went public, Fetterman began speaking out about his battle with depression, revealing details from the past few years of his struggle. Fetterman was met with "an outpouring of goodwill" from "his colleagues and the public alike" (Ball 2023). He returned to the Senate on April 17, and continues to be outspoken as a mental health advocate. However, in contrast to Eagleton, there was no media storm, and what news coverage did exist was generally positive and supportive of his treatment.

The parallel between these cases is not exact, of course; both involve sitting Senators, but only Eagleton was running for vice president, giving his story more heat to boost it to a media storm. However, the amount of fuel present for each story played a prominent role. The dramatic difference in the amount and type of coverage their cases received reflects the changing landscape and views of mental health in the ensuing fifty years since the so-called Thomas Eagleton affair (Purcell 2023). There simply wasn't the same amount of fuel available in 2023 as there was in 1972 for a story about a politician's struggles with depression to catch hold in the media. Since the 1970s, the stigma surrounding mental health issues has notably decreased, as struggles like depression are increasingly seen as more commonplace. When Eagleton dropped out of the vice presidential race in 1972, antidepressants had not been invented. By 2018, over 13% of adults in the US reported taking antidepressants (Brody and Gu 2020). Today, over one in five adults in the US report living with a mental illness, and it is not unprecedented for prominent and respected individuals to be vocal about their struggles. By 2023, when news of Fetterman's depression broke, it was much more culturally acceptable to struggle with a mental illness, including and especially depression.

The contrasting public and media responses to Thomas Eagleton's and John Fetterman's mental health struggles underscore how societal changes and temporal context can alter the fuel (as well as the heat) of media coverage on similar issues across different eras.

Fuel Example 2: Boeing Crash in 2018 versus Boeing Crash in 2019

On October 29, 2018, Lion Air Flight 610, a Boeing 737 Max 8 jet, departed from Tangerang, Indonesia. Thirteen minutes after takeoff, the airplane crashed into the Java Sea, killing all 189 people on board (181 passengers, 6 cabin crew members, and 2 pilots). Although this tragedy did not involve Americans, the sudden and complete loss of life made it potentially newsworthy for the US media, and the heat of the event was amplified by the fact that thirty-eight of the passengers killed were Indonesian civil servants, including three judges on Indonesia's High Court and National Court. Yet US news coverage barely covered the crash, with just forty-five national newspaper articles in the week following the crash.[15] In the following weeks, it became clear that the cause of the crash was the malfunction of a new flight-control system – one that Boeing

---

[15] Based on a search of ProQuest archives of U.S. Major Dailies (as described in Section 3), using the search string "(Lion OR Boeing) AND flight AND 610."

had not disclosed to airlines or to pilots. This automated system, called MCAS, had pushed the nose of the Lion Air Flight 610 plane down as the pilots continued to try to pull it up. Still, US news coverage did not pick up the story in earnest, with coverage never rising above the week following the crash.

Barely four months later, on March 10, 2019, another Boeing 737 Max 8 jet, Ethiopian Airlines Flight 302, departed from Addis Ababa, Ethiopia. Six minutes after takeoff, the airplane crashed, killing all 157 people on board (149 passengers, 6 cabin crew, and 2 pilots). Among the passengers were twenty-two people affiliated with the United Nations in some way. In the days that followed, it became clear that a malfunction of the MCAS flight-control system was again to blame. In isolation, the tragedy of Ethiopian Airlines Flight 302 was arguably not dramatically more newsworthy than the earlier crash of Lion Air Flight 610 (although the fact that Americans were killed in the Flight 302 crash increased its perceived news value). Yet it prompted a swift and strong media storm, with 351 national US news articles printed in the week following the crash.[16]

A big difference with the second of these two crashes is that, well, it came second. Whereas the first crash was a seemingly isolated data point, the second crash suggested a pattern. Notably, the media storm erupted immediately following the second crash, whereas it took most governments around the world days to reach the decision to halt the flight of additional Boeing 737 Max jets. In the US, the Federal Aviation Administration (FAA) decided to ground the 737 Max jets on March 13, three days into the media storm. In other words, the media storm following the second crash was not due merely to the additional oxygen provided by government agencies (although that subsequent oxygen helped heighten and extend the media storm); government agencies, including the FAA, had also weighed in on the earlier Lion Air Flight crash. Rather, the second crash was more relevant to journalists and readers because of the notion of *systemic* malfunction laid by the first crash. It was also easier for news outlets to write about the second crash, having already devoted some journalistic resources to getting up to speed on the details of the first crash. In short, the media storm following the crash of Ethiopian Airlines Flight 302 occurred not only because of the heat of the event and the oxygen of governmental attention but was also fueled by the different context in which it occurred.

Oxygen

Fires are sustained when burning fuel "reacts with oxygen from the surrounding air, releasing heat and generating combustion products (gases, smoke, embers,

---

[16] Based on a search of ProQuest archives of U.S. Major Dailies (as described in Section 3), using the search string "(Ethiopian OR Boeing) AND flight AND (737 OR 302)."

etc.)" (Bear 2019). For media storms, the oxygen takes two forms: first, the attention available from the media to be given to this or any other news item in the first place (i.e., the current agenda capacity of the news industry), and second, the attention the item receives from other actors outside traditional news, reinforcing continued and increased media attention.

For the first form of oxygen, when other major news items are consuming the media agenda, it decreases the likelihood that a media storm will erupt. Imagine, for example, that Ruth Bader Ginsburg's death occurred not before a presidential election, serving as fuel to frame her death in terms of an upcoming electoral mandate, but rather on the heels of a major event such as the terrorist attacks of September 11, 2001. Ginsburg's death would of course still have been covered in the news. But her death likely would have received much less attention not only because of the lack of relevant fuel in current conditions (i.e., an upcoming election) but also because following a major event like a domestic terrorist attack the oxygen of the media environment is largely consumed by coverage of that major event, leaving little available oxygen for anything else. Generally speaking, the national media only has enough oxygen to support one major storm at a time (Atkinson, Lovett, and Baumgartner 2014), not unlike how an explosion tends to consume all the oxygen in the immediate vicinity, often extinguishing other smaller fires nearby.

But the second is the more prominent form of oxygen in our model: the attention given to the news item by political actors beyond journalists – really anyone outside the news itself, from politicians to celebrities, corporate entities to late-night talk show hosts and everyone else. When a sitting member of Congress or a Hollywood star talks about a current event during an interview, when a business references it in a television ad, when people talk about it on Twitter, when social protests form in the streets ... all that attention serves as oxygen, fanning the flames of media coverage. Items in the news ricochet through the media environment, including daytime "soft news" shows like *The View* and comedic/satirical shows like *Saturday Night Live* and late-night talk shows. Amplification from these shows feeds back into "hard" news coverage and can play an outsized role in putting news items on the public's radar (Baum 2005). Politicians, in particular, often have incentives to weigh in on the discussion unfolding in the media, such as wanting to remind their constituents and fellow party members of the politician's engagement with the issue. Journalists, in turn, have strong incentives to quote, or "index," these political voices (Bennett 1990). Other times, these same political actors have incentives to pull oxygen away from a growing news item, when that item would not benefit them, and instead employ "wag the dog" communication strategies.

As discussed in Section 5, for policy activists (including established interest groups, grassroots organizations, and everyone in between) who *want* news coverage of their issue, namely because they want the current policy surrounding a given issue to change, there is strong incentive to draw attention to news items that advance their cause. These activists know that the more public attention it receives, the more newsworthy it will become, feeding a positive feedback loop of attention. For these activists, it does not take a major event and a subsequent media storm to prompt their amplification. For example, the Million Moms March to call for more gun control legislation took place on Mother's Day in 2000, a full year after Columbine and during a lull in media coverage of the issue. But when a media storm erupts, these groups direct even more energy to amplifying the story through press conferences and the like.

By contrast, for policy activists who prefer the status quo policy, the best news coverage tends to be no news coverage (Schattschneider 1960). After a mass shooting, for example, gun control activists amp up their messaging even louder and lobby news outlets to give the event even more coverage (Rogowski and Tucker 2019). But activists who generally oppose gun control, such as the NRA, are more likely to stay publicly quiet, targeting their messaging at their supporters only and waiting for the news cycle to die down. In this regard, we can also think of both forms of oxygen in terms of headwinds (pushing back against a story) and tailwinds (adding a boost to a story in bursting into a media storm).

In our digitally connected world, the rapid dissemination of information plays a pivotal role in the formation of media storms. A single piece of news can traverse the digital landscape at an unprecedented pace, reaching far and wide as it is shared across platforms. Social media amplifies narratives, and when an event captivates content developers and users, it holds the potential to intensify a media storm. The convergence of hashtags, trending topics, and user-generated content can create a perfect storm of online engagement that propels a story into the collective consciousness, helping prompt a media storm in the traditional news.

Turning again to the case of police use of deadly force, both forms of oxygen as we have defined them helped contribute to the media storms following Michael Brown's murder in 2014 and George Floyd's murder in 2020. First, both events occurred during a relative lull in breaking news (recall that by May of 2020 most people were in some form of pandemic lockdown, but with scarce new news about the pandemic to report). There was, in other words, plenty of available oxygen in the media environment available to spend on each of these stories. Applying a thought experiment similar to the one we proposed with Justice Ginsburg, imagine that Michael Brown or George Floyd had been murdered in March 2020 (only months before Floyd was actually killed), during the frantic surge of news about the global pandemic. Their deaths would still have made the news, but it's much less likely that most Americans would know their names.

Second, both events received massive amounts of amplification from beyond the news media. For instance, in 2014, the topics that received the most US-based Twitter attention were the death of Eric Garner from a police chokehold, the fatal shooting of Michael Brown, and the Ferguson protests (including a surge in the use of #BlackLivesMatter) – far outpacing the volume of tweets about major events like the US Supreme Court's landmark *Burwell* v. *Hobby Lobby* ruling and Russia's annexing of Crimea (Echelon Insights 2014). In 2020, the use of #BlackLivesMatter hashtag outpaced more than tenfold the attention it had received in 2014 (Anderson et al. 2020).

Oxygen Example 1: Brock Turner versus Finn Wolff

In January of 2015, Stanford student Brock Turner, then nineteen, sexually assaulted a woman outside a fraternity party, while she lay unconscious. Two students biking nearby caught sight of the attack, tackled Turner, and turned him in to authorities. Turner pleaded not guilty to the several charges he was indicted for, including rape, felony sexual assault, and attempted rape. In June 2016, he was sentenced to prison, although the time served was eventually lightened due to good behavior.

Just a couple years later, a similar incident took place at UC Berkeley, where student Finn Wolff was charged with sexual assault against two women. The first woman, Jane Doe 1, testified that on a frat "date night" in November of 2017, he groped her and grabbed her roughly, leaving bruises and scratches over her body, and later raped her in an empty room. The year following the attack, she informed several of the fraternity's officers, none of whom took action. A second woman, Jane Doe 2, accused Wolff of forcing her to perform oral sex on him. In 2019, both women took the issue to court, and the judge ruled in their favor. Wolff was charged with two counts of misdemeanor battery, and felony assault with force. In 2022, all felony charges were dropped after both Jane Doe witnesses admitted to numerous falsities.

Although important details varied, the cases are similar in that both Turner and Wolff were students at elite universities in northern California accused of sexual assault in the post-MeToo era. Yet only one (the Turner case) caught fire in the news. Why? We suspect a major reason is that the survivor in the Turner case, now self-identified as Chanel Miller, released the "victim impact statement" she had read during Turner's trial to BuzzFeed news. BuzzFeed published the statement, and it went viral, gaining widespread publicity for the case (Baker 2016). This public attention, largely via social media, fanned the flames of the case, providing oxygen for the media storm surrounding Turner. It is worth noting that the Wolff accusations happened *after* the media storm surrounding Turner, reinforcing the idea that fuel alone (in this case, recent relevant media coverage) is not sufficient to prompt a media storm.

Oxygen Example 2: Flint, MI versus Newark NJ

In 2014, the city of Flint, Michigan, facing a $25 million budget deficit, switched its water source from Detroit's water system to the Flint River to cut costs. Unbeknownst to city officials, the corrosive, unfiltered water from the river drew toxic lead from already dilapidated pipes. The water was foul and discolored, but citizen protests in the Black-majority area failed to draw national attention. City officials responded by dumping large amounts of disinfectant into the water system, which resulted in such a high chloride content in the water that the local General Motors automotive plant stopped using the water after realizing it was corroding engine parts. The poisoned water led to high blood lead levels in children, posing dangers to their growth and development. In January 2015, Flint citizens and the local city council escalated their complaints to the Environmental Protection Agency (EPA), which then began an investigation. Michigan's Department of Environmental Quality dismissed the complaints and the EPA's investigation, and little was done to correct the rising issues. In late 2015, researchers from Virginia Tech and a local doctor, Dr. Mona Hanna-Attiasha, led studies testing water samples and children's lead levels that confirmed the alarming levels of lead in the water and in the children's blood. These findings were amplified on social media by political actors, celebrities, and citizens, and by the end of 2015 the state of Michigan finally responded by declaring a state of emergency, distributing bottled water, and switching back to Detroit's water system. However, the lead pipes continued to be an issue, and the water remained unsafe. Citizens of Flint, along with several advocacy groups like the ACLU and the Natural Resources Defense Council (NRDC), took the issue to federal court under the Safe Drinking Water Act. President Obama declared the crisis a federal emergency in January 2016, and finally a media storm erupted (Figure 6 chronicles the timeline of the storm). The media storm prompted a celebrity benefit concert, and President Obama visited in May 2016 after receiving a letter from the young activist, Mari Copeny (see Figure 3 for a comparison of Copeny with Greta Thunberg). In November 2016, three years after the initial water diversion, a federal judge ruled for the plaintiffs and ordered that the state give bottled water to Flint's residents. In March 2017, the state officially funded the city's replacement of pipes, though this would take nearly a decade to complete. Many education and health programs were implemented to help residents deal with trauma and the health implications of the crisis, and criminal charges were brought against several state officials (though they were eventually dropped). Civil cases for damages continued into the next decade, and although a landmark settlement of $626 million was announced in 2021, affected citizens have yet to receive settlement monies as of 2025.

Citizens in Newark, New Jersey, faced a similar reality when the EPA found elevated levels of lead in water pipes, heavily impacting pregnant women and children. The issue had been a problem since at least 2016 but was only addressed on the federal level in 2018. A year later the city was ordered to distribute water filters to 19,000 homes, and when the filters caused bacterial growth, bottled water was delivered to affected households. The situation was taken to federal court, with the Newark Education Workers Caucus and the NRDC demanding that safe drinking water be made available to citizens and the pipes replaced as soon as possible. The lead pipes were mostly replaced by the city with copper pipes by 2021.

Only one of these water safety hazards (Flint) prompted a media storm. In this case, the media storm occurred years after the problems in the Flint water system started, after the problem received small bursts of attention from different sections of the media ecosystem, until finally the item caught the attention of the national news. One key difference was the oxygen in the Flint case, provided by interested actors, including researchers, a local doctor, the federal government, and filmmaker Michael Moore. The initial crisis in Flint also happened during the same time as Michael Brown's death in Ferguson in 2014 and the media storm (and activism by citizens) surrounding his murder, which pointed to the many racial disparities in attention to issues in majority Black cities in the Midwest. This timing may have helped elevate the problems in Flint to media prominence, giving the story a narrative fuel that helped offset the otherwise perceived low newsworthiness of a predominantly low-income, Black community.

In the case of Newark, little oxygen was released in the form of activists' posting on social media or a federal response, thus dampening chances of a media storm. However, Newark city officials and the federal government acted much more quickly, likely because of the earlier media storm surrounding Flint. This case points to the positive spillover effects media storms can have, prompting swifter preventative actions by political actors down the road. As newspaper publisher and politician Joseph Pulitzer is reported to have said, "More crime, immorality and rascality is prevented by the fear of exposure in the newspapers than by all the laws, morals and statutes ever devised" (Daly 2012).[17]

7 Effects of Media Storms

In this final section, we reiterate that understanding the forces required to produce a media storm matters because media storms matter. Whether the results are fleeting or more durable, every media storm we have examined and validated has produced some sort of effect. We simply cannot find a single example of a media storm that had no effect at all, and we challenge the reader to think of counterexamples.

In some cases, it's clear that a media storm was almost exclusively responsible for any changes and effects that followed, since in the absence of the media storm, people would not have known about the underlying event. Examples here include the Catholic church abuse scandal, the #MeToo sexual assault movement, and the Flint, Michigan water crisis. In other cases, it's clear that a large part of the effects following a media storm were a result of the underlying event itself, but likely exacerbated or expedited by the media storm. Examples here include Hurricane Katrina, the COVID-19 pandemic, and the economic recession that began in 2007. Although each of these events would have had real-life impacts even in the unthinkable scenario of the event not becoming a media storm, the size and duration of the resulting media storm, along with how the media storm framed the event, undoubtedly had an impact as well.

Importantly, not all the effects of media storms align with those we might naively expect based on the direction in which the political winds of a media storm initially blow. Sometimes, even though a media storm overwhelmingly supports a particular perspective (e.g., #BlackLivesMatter), the effects can serve to double down on the opposite perspective (e.g., #BlueLivesMatter). At other times, the effects of a media storm can be directionally in line with the political winds of a media storm (e.g., increased requirements and funding for police to wear body cameras) and yet that effect may fall short of the advocated outcome (e.g., body cameras have been shown to be largely ineffective at reducing police use of violence (Yokum, Ravishankar, and Coppock 2019)).

Building on classic agenda-setting scholarship – which shows that the salience of topics in the media directly influences what the public and political decision-makers consider important (McCombs and Shaw 1972) – we focus in this section on three key (often overlapping) agenda areas: (1) communication effects (i.e., changes in the extent to which news outlets, government, corporations, and/or average people talk about – and how they frame – an item as

---

[17] Rascality!

a result of a media storm), (2) cultural zeitgeist effects (i.e., changes in how the issue or event is understood culturally by people in the US and beyond as a result of a media storm), and (3) policy effects (i.e., changes in rules, laws, or policies at any level of government or for organizations, companies, etc., as a result of a media storm). As the examples we will offer make clear, often the effects of a media storm ripple across two or all three of these interconnected agenda areas. In each case, media storms can operate akin to Kingdon's (2010) windows of opportunity, wherein the previous equilibrium can be disrupted, replaced with a new status quo. We also consider how these windows of opportunity can serve as a learning platform for future activists, politicians, policymakers, and even celebrities. We discuss how storm fronts help set the stage for an incoming media storm. Finally, we end with thoughts about lingering questions for future research, including applications of the fire triangle model in the context of other media systems.

Agenda-Setting Effects of Media Storms

Communication Effects

Most media storms will include communication effects, increasing the attention given to the event/issue by political actors, including the general public, and often reshaping that discourse in how the news media frame the event/issue. Even relatively small and short-lived media storms can have these kinds of communication effects. For example, in 2009, parents in Ft. Collins, CO, claimed their six-year-old son became trapped inside a huge silver helium balloon and was carried off into the atmosphere. Their claim was accompanied by a gripping video showing a big balloon shaped like a flying saucer zooming through the air; soon the video was plastered on news channels throughout the world. This event (known as the "Balloon Boy" incident) finally ended when it became clear that it was a hoax by the child's parents in a bid for viral attention. Yet, even after the media storm died down, there was much discussion about how much the hoax cost in terms of resources and time when attempting a rescue, as well as social introspection about the risks of mis- and disinformation (although those terms had not yet become popular). Many said it was a wake-up call for the media not to follow every shiny object and to create a better vetting process for stories in the rising age of social media. As one scholar put it, "more intense fact-checking is desperately needed in this post-Survivor world where 'reality' is a form of cheap entertainment" (Amster 2010). Although the rise of mis- and disinformation and questions of how the news media should cover those stories has only gotten more fraught (Aeon 2021; Lazer et al. 2018), the Balloon Boy media storm helped lay the seeds for what would become a much bigger cultural reckoning.

More profound media storms can have even more powerful communication effects. Mass shootings, for example, often have gripping communication effects, with immediate responses from local officials and calls for reform at the federal level, amplified by demands for action from impassioned activists. For example, the media storm following the mass shooting at Columbine High School in Colorado in 1999 began to change the way the media communicates about gun ownership and shootings and, specifically, how journalists reference shootings (Birkland and Lawrence 2009).

Some media storms we might expect to have major policy consequences fall short in that arena but still impact the public agenda. Consider, for example, the media storms that have followed major climate change events (e.g., the 1997 Kyoto Protocol to reduce greenhouse gas emissions, or Hurricane Helene in 2024). Since long-term changes in climate policy, attitudes, and behavior depend on public receptivity and political follow-through, the effects of these media storms can falter under economic and cultural pressures (e.g., backlash or apathy) and a lack of political appetite (e.g., pulling out of the Paris Accords in 2017 and again in 2025). These countercurrents can undermine long-term changes that are directionally aligned with the signals of a media storm surrounding climate change, resulting in a slog and a frustrating attention cycle for activists in that issue space as they race against time (Bergquist and Warshaw 2019; Druckman and McGrath 2019; Kotcher et al. 2021). Although these climate change media storms yielded scarce, if any lasting policy change, they made a substantive and important impact on the public conversation surrounding climate change.

Returning to our running example of police use of deadly force, when the media spotlights turned toward this issue in 2014 and 2020, following the deaths of Michael Brown and George Floyd, respectively, public opinion appears to have moved in tandem, reflecting substantive and measurable agenda effects. A poll in April 2015, for example, found that 92% of Americans favored requiring on-duty police officers to wear video cameras (Shackford 2016). Note that we cannot compare this data point to public opinion prior to Brown's death, since to the best of our knowledge there were no polls prior to Brown's death that asked the public about police body cameras. The very existence of public opinion data on this question in 2015 (and in several subsequent surveys since 2015) represents the effect of the media storm following Brown's death. And following the 2020 spike in coverage during the media storm surrounding George Floyd's death, the percentage of White Americans believing that police are more likely to use excessive force against a Black culprit nearly doubled, from 25% in 2016 to 49% in 2020 (Monmouth 2020). The public alarm influenced companies, too, especially in 2020. Twitter posted billboards around the country displaying tweets in support of the Black Lives Matter movement (The Drum 2020).[18] Companies including the NBA, Old Navy, and Papa John's Pizza produced BLM-supportive ads. Through communication effects, media storms are rare windows of opportunity for changing hearts and minds, along with corporate priorities.

Cultural Zeitgeist Effects

Cultural zeitgeist effects emerge when a media storm alters the broader narratives, symbols, and shared meanings that society associates with an issue, long after headlines fade. Even for those media storms that have no lasting policy impacts, they can leave an enduring imprint on how people remember and talk about events, turning them into cultural touchstones. For example, the so-called Miracle on the Hudson, where Captain Chesley "Sully" Sullenberger safely landed a passenger plane in the Hudson River in 2009 and saved all passengers after a bird strike, prompted a media storm and even spawned a successful movie starring Tom Hanks. There were numerous investigations in its wake, but there weren't any enduring effects as far as aviation safety policies, responses to bird strikes, or changing the way crashes were framed in the media (Minutaglio 2019). Ultimately, it was a feel-good story that justifiably became well-known for heroics but made little impact otherwise except, again, a lasting and therefore meaningful imprint on the cultural conversation.

Media storms that *do* have major policy effects can also have meaningful effects on the cultural zeitgeist. For example, the Watergate scandal that began in 1972 is best known for leading to President Nixon's resignation and to campaign finance policy reform. But the term "Watergate" (after the Watergate Hotel where members of Nixon's campaign broke into the Democratic National Committee headquarters) lodged so strongly into public discourse that the suffix "-gate" has now become a shorthand for a scandal.

Sometimes the cultural zeitgeist effects of a media storm can manifest in multiple competing directions, signaling a backlash effect. Black Lives Matter exemplifies how a media storm can ignite far-reaching cultural shifts, reshaping public discourse and beliefs around race and justice in ways that endure beyond immediate policy debates. At the same time, the movement's visibility prompted strong counternarratives, which reveal how cultural backlash can arise even amid heightened awareness. Such backlash is vividly exemplified by the emergence of hashtags such as #AllLivesMatter and #BlueLivesMatter in response to the #BlackLivesMatter movement. These hashtags, and the people and groups proffering them on social media, faced vehement opposition and backlash, particularly within the Black community, as they were interpreted

---

[18] www.thedrum.com/creative-works/project/twitter-twitter-black-lives-matter-billboards.

as both rejecting the #BlackLivesMatter movement and endorsing racist sentiments. This backlash underscored the persistence of the belief that Black lives are not widely valued, emphasizing the ongoing need for movements like #BlackLivesMatter (Brown, Block, and Stout 2020; Cowart, Blackstone, and Riley 2022).

Policy Effects

Many media storms also yield what are arguably larger and longer-term consequences through their impact on public policy itself. An example of durable policy effects is the case of the #FreeBritney media storm. Although most people following that media storm at the time focused only on Britney Spears' personal case, the media storm had a wider-reaching influence than at first look. Several laws in California were changed as a result, increasing the transparency of conservatorships, limiting the power of the conservator, and easing the process of extricating someone from a conservatorship (Wiener 2021).

As with communication and cultural zeitgeist effects, the long-term policy effects of a media storm do not always match the political winds of the initial media storm. For example, following the 1999 Columbine High School shooting, bills were introduced in Congress to close the gun show loophole, where some of the guns in the massacre had been purchased, and to require stricter background checks. Yet, while some laws were passed affirming already-in-place laws banning the sale of guns to criminals and minors, the background checks bill was passed in the US Senate but not the House. Other policies were put in place by individual schools and districts in response to Columbine, including installing metal detectors, instituting backpack searches, and other restrictions. And new organizations began to mobilize for more gun control. But notably, along with the loss of passing a stricter background check bill, in 2004 Congress declined to renew the Federal Assault Weapons Ban (which was in place at the time of the Columbine shooting). In many ways, as school shootings have become more common over time, the pendulum has swung against gun control, with a backlash response, including the NRA becoming more militant about supporting Second Amendment rights, as well as the Supreme Court affirming a fundamental right to own a gun in *District of Columbia v. Heller* in 2008 (Rogowski and Tucker 2019). Exemplifying this swing, in the last two and a half decades, even as incidents of mass shootings have become more common, public support for gun control has waned (Newman and Hartman 2019; Rogowski and Tucker 2019). Still, the Columbine tragedy remains an important symbolic touchstone for activists and advocacy groups lobbying for gun control (a cultural zeitgeist effect).

One notable way that media storms can have policy effects is via *policy diffusion*, whereby a policy in one region (e.g., a city or state) can influence the way that similar regions consider and approach the same issue, often driven in part by public appetite (Pacheco 2012). Take the example of recreational marijuana legalization in 2012 in Colorado. On November 6, 2012, Colorado voters approved a constitutional amendment leading to the functional legalization of marijuana for recreational use in the state. Colorado was thus one of the first two states to legalize recreational marijuana (Washington voters also legalized recreational marijuana the same year). In an example of a media storm surrounding an anticipated event, a media storm surrounded the first retail recreational marijuana store opening in Colorado on January 1, 2014 – which media outlets called "Green Wednesday." News outlets like the *New York Times* reported that consumers were lined up around the block before dawn (Healy 2014). In this wave of coverage, the media changed the way it communicated to the public about marijuana, shifting from framing the issue in terms of criminal or illicit use or even medicinal health care to framing it in terms of tax revenue and economic success – a frame made more salient by (i.e., tapping into the fuel of) the post-2008 recession economic conditions. Other states saw the economic successes of Colorado (and Washington) as evidenced by this media storm, making it easier for states to adopt similar policies (Shipan and Volden 2008). Voters in Alaska, Oregon, and Washington, DC legalized marijuana in 2014, and many more followed suit in 2016, including California, Maine, Massachusetts, and Nevada; as of this writing, twenty-four states have legalized some form of recreational use of marijuana. It's possible that this type of policy diffusion would have happened in the absence of the 2014 media storm, but it surely would not have happened as fast. This media storm arguably completed the long shift away from communicating about marijuana in negative terms to one more benign and economically beneficial, altering the public agenda as well as having durable policy effects.

Our running example of police use of deadly force is another example of a media storm with policy effects, including counterintuitive effects that may not be apparent until many years down the road. The media storm sparked by the 2014 killing of Michael Brown led to several policy changes, specifically surrounding police use of body cameras. The US Department of Justice provided more than $184 million in funding for police body cameras. Between 2014 and 2018, the number of US states requiring police officers to use body cameras increased from zero to five, and the number that provide legislated funding for the purchase and maintenance of police body cameras increased from zero to fourteen (NCSL 2021). As Politico reports: "By 2016, nearly half of 15,328 law enforcement agencies across the country, and 80% of police departments with more than 500 officers, had begun using the cameras, according to the Department of Justice. For many police officers in America today, body cameras are standard-issue equipment that they are supposed to turn on during most law enforcement activities" (Farooq 2024). In June of 2020 alone, thirty-two state governments introduced 317 pieces of legislation or executive orders aimed at addressing police use of force (NCSL 2021). At the time, these policy changes were lauded as a big win for Black Lives Matter activists, but when evaluated over the long term, they seem not to have had the desired effect of decreasing deaths at the hands of police. In the years since these policy changes, many studies have shown that body cameras have done little to curb the violence and police killings of Black people or others (Lum et al. 2019; Yokum, Ravishankar, and Coppock 2019). In fact, police have become more heavily militarized since the rise of and in response to Black Lives Matter (Simpson 2024), and adopted new technologies that have been shown to introduce further biases against non-White people, including facial recognition software (Fowler 2020; Johnson and Johnson 2020).

Media Storms as Platforms for Activism and Political Learning

Media storms often serve as more than just fleeting headlines; they become stages where new tactics are showcased, and emerging leaders gain visibility. By spotlighting new strategies or gaffes in real time, a media storm can function as a live classroom, teaching politicians how to agenda set, teaching celebrities how to weigh in (or stay silent) on unfolding debates, and – our focus here – teaching organizers how to frame messages, mobilize supporters, and build networks.

An example of a media storm that served an educational role in political activism was the Occupy Wall Street Movement that swept the country and the globe in 2011–12. Although it seemed to start with a bang and end in a fizzle, it ended up having long-term effects both culturally (e.g., the framing of what constitutes protesting) and in its direct influence on activism and activists in general. There had been sit-ins in the 1960s to protest the war in Vietnam, with activists occupying administrative buildings on college campuses, but the practice of setting up large-scale encampments was not a common tactic. In 2011, when the Occupy activists sought to protest the negative effects of income inequality and capitalism, they created a new kind of protest strategy by pitching tents and digging in for a long haul with an occupation of public areas and the creation of a temporary cooperative community (Gupta 2024). Starting in New York City near the statue of the Bull of Wall Street, the Occupy Movement spread all over the country, from Washington, DC to Oakland, CA, and in between, and to other countries worldwide. It seemed to end with no discernible effect on income inequality, with no policy changes or laws being passed – and the gap between rich and poor has only gotten more pronounced in the years following (Kealy 2021).

However, the Occupy Movement – and, more pointedly, the media storm that covered it – was influential in sparking the encampment phase of the Arab Spring Movement in 2011–12, as the two movements happened at nearly the same time and influenced each other. The Arab Spring Movement helped to topple governments in Tunisia and Egypt (Yangfang 2012), though many countries where the Arab Spring occurred have reverted to authoritarian regimes (Sadiki and Saleh 2023), another counterintuitive policy effect. For many leaders of other social movements centering on social, racial, and climate justice, the Occupy Movement was how they started and learned their craft or were otherwise inspired to activate, including DeRay Mckesson of Black Lives Matter (Young and Leszczynski 2021). In short, the Occupy Movement and the media storm that gave it an audience fundamentally changed the way activism and protest are practiced in the US and beyond, adding a new disruptive tool to the toolkit of activists worldwide protesting a variety of issues. There is a direct throughline from the Occupy Movement to the encampments beginning in 2024 on college campuses protesting the Israel–Hamas war in Gaza; this "student movement follows in the footsteps of Occupy Wall Street" (Gupta 2024).

In a similar vein, the media storm following the Parkland, Florida high school mass shooting in 2018 served as a powerful learning moment with durable effects, arguably in all three agenda-setting categories we have examined. Young survivors of this shooting created an enduring advocacy organization, March for Our Lives, working to mobilize young people to vote and to support stricter gun control policy measures. While voting rates of youth have gone up and down in the years since the shooting (Bump 2023), several of the youth organizers and survivors have gone on to be important political actors in their own right, including Maxwell Alejandro Frost, the twice-elected Florida representative and Congress' youngest member, and David Hogg, a DNC member who ran for vice chair in 2024. Even if the direct effects of the Parkland shooting media storm on the issue of gun control wane in future years, the rise and elections of these two young political actors – fostered not only by the Parkland tragedy but also by the media storm that followed – will continue to have real effects into the future.

Reshaping the Issue Landscape: The Importance of Storm Fronts

The last aspect of media storm effects we want to consider is the influence that a surge in media coverage can have on the issue landscape itself. While we have focused on media storms as agents of change, the near-miss news items that gain a sudden amount of coverage but at a level that doesn't quite make it to media storm status – what we call *storm fronts* – often lay the groundwork for future media storms and also alert the attention of media ecosystems and journalists on the hunt for needed scoops. In this way, storm fronts not only provide fuel for future media coverage but also restructure the entire environment in a way that makes the landscape more hospitable to all three elements (heat, fuel, and oxygen) and, thus, future fires. For example, turning again to the case of police use of force, there were thousands of unarmed Black people killed by police in the years leading up to Michael Brown's death in 2014, whose stories never made it to the level of a media storm. Yet the media storm following Michael Brown's death would surely not have been as large (or might not even have become a media storm at all) were it not for those earlier tragedies. In addition to providing fuel in the form of some amount of earlier relevant news coverage, these deaths mobilized families, communities, and journalists for years. They built organizations to challenge and combat the violence, elevate their cases, and push back against the narrative that had cast these victims as just criminals and therefore unworthy of sympathy or cast police as justified (Brown, Block, and Stout 2020). These many cases presented in the news as a series of storm fronts (e.g., Freddie Gray's death in 2015), helping shape the landscape for future media storms.

In this regard, sometimes it can seem like storm fronts (and even media storms) make little impact until they do. In issue areas in which there has been seemingly little movement or effects from media storms or storm fronts for many years, things can suddenly turn in one direction or another. For example, consider smoking and tobacco use. For more than seventy years, very little policy movement toward limiting the use of tobacco seemed possible, despite decades of news coverage about the health risks of tobacco, including a media storm in 1964 after the Surgeon General came out against smoking (Baumgartner and Jones 2009). And then, suddenly, in the 1990s, the dam broke. A new wave of storm fronts and media storms erupted, centered mostly on federal court decisions to hold tobacco companies accountable for health issues caused by their products and for deliberately concealing evidence showing that they had long known about the harmful effects of smoking. These legal actions – and the media coverage that followed – resulted in public marketing bans, massive financial settlements, and billions of dollars dedicated to mitigating the societal impact of smoking. These court decisions, and the surrounding media coverage that followed, led to significant policy changes (e.g., state-level bans on indoor smoking) and a sharp decline in cigarette smoking in the US and other countries (Chapman 2021; Pacheco 2012).

But that timeline would have looked very different were it not for the decades of media coverage (including the 1964 media storm) that came first.

A final example of how media storms and storm fronts can have larger effects in terms of policy change and diffusion, communication and framing, the cultural zeitgeist, and the overall political landscape is that of same-sex marriage. This issue ignited multiple media storms and a number of storm fronts in early 2004 when President Bush, under pressure from religious groups, came out in support of a constitutional amendment against gay marriage. Later that same year, another set of storm fronts and media storms hit when San Francisco began to issue same-sex marriage licenses and Massachusetts legalized same-sex marriage – perhaps both as a backlash against President Bush's proposed constitutional ban on gay marriage. After several years of storm fronts around the push and pull of legal battles, policy diffusion began in 2008 when states began adopting Massachusetts' example, including New York and Washington, and a round of media storms began in 2012 when President Obama came out in favor of same-sex marriage. The Supreme Court began deliberations in 2013 on the constitutionality of the Defense of Marriage Act, passed by President Clinton in 1996, throwing out parts of it as unconstitutional. On June 26, 2015, the Court ruled that same-sex couples have the right to marry in *Obergefell* v. *Hodges*, igniting yet another media storm. In short, policy diffusion bubbled up from state to the federal level in just over ten years, which is lightning speed in terms of policy change. The media storms and fronts in 2004 thus created new ways of framing the issue, namely in terms of injustice for same-sex couples in light of President Bush's opposition (Becker 2012). The cultural zeitgeist had for many years been influenced by depictions of gay people in Hollywood and in high-profile celebrities coming out (e.g., Ellen DeGeneres). Together, these forces opened the window of change wider for activists who had been advocating for same-sex marriage for many decades, with public opinion following swiftly (Pew Research 2013). Between 2004 and 2014, public support for same-sex marriage in the US grew dramatically, rising from 31% in 2004 to 55% in 2014 (Pew Research 2019). The media storms aided in pushing the issue across the finish line in terms of federal policy, framing and communication, and the cultural zeitgeist, including public support, which by 2018 reached 67% (Pew Research 2019).

Questions and Future Research

In this short Element, we have endeavored to deconstruct the components of a media storm, unpacking the necessary and only jointly sufficient conditions for an event to catch fire in the news. But many questions remain. For example, do the levels of heat, fuel, and oxygen tend to vary between accidental media storms and institutional/anticipated media storms? Has the proliferation of social media and new technology reduced the opportunity costs for journalists deciding to chase a story and, thus, increased the frequency of media storms? For activists in a given issue space, how advantageous is igniting a media storm versus working under the radar? Are some issue areas more prone to a backlash response than others (thinking of our example of gun control)?

One avenue of research that would likely require its own volume would be taking a deep dive into how and under what conditions media storms act as policy windows of opportunity. Is it because the media storm offers an opportunity to change the way an issue is framed, or is it something more structural in the way that resources are diverted to those issue areas? Future research could examine the dynamics of framing an event before, during, and after a media storm to better understand the ways in which the media changes how they communicate about an issue, and whether a new frame used during a media storm tends sticks in future news coverage or whether the dominant narrative tends to revert back to the pre-storm equilibrium.

We can also envision research studies that delve further into the three elements of our fire triangle model, including conjoint experiments where respondents are exposed to different versions of a media storm, where one of the elements is higher or lower compared to the others, to isolate the relative effect of each. Other observational studies might further break down the three elements of heat, fuel, and oxygen into a molecular view of their relative dynamics, comparing how media storms unfold via social media versus legacy media and citizen journalists versus professional journalists, as well as partisan versus nonpartisan sources. Many of these structures are in flux, so understanding how they work will be important for journalists looking to break a new scoop, activists working in these issue areas, and everyday people to be discerning as far as understanding how media dynamics can play out, shaping their perceptions of reality.

Perhaps the most important avenue of future research will be testing the media storm fire triangle model in the comparative context of other media systems beyond the US. Although we understand the phenomenon of media storms to be a human phenomenon, present in any media system, there are several factors that should affect the *rate* at which media storms occur and their *volatility*. Focusing in particular on the variables Hallin and Mancini discuss in their canonical work comparing democratic media systems (2004), we see two factors as particularly important for future research: the structure of the media market and the consensus versus majoritarian nature of the democracy. In line with comparative research on game framing, we expect that media systems with more marketplace competition will generally yield media storms that are both more frequent and more volatile (i.e., that tend to erupt at a higher volume of coverage, but with less predictable durations) (Schmuck et al. 2017). The logic here is that marketplace competition – in the form of a splintered traditional media system and/or an active hybrid media system (Chadwick 2017) – accelerates journalistic dynamics of lurching to and then congregating around the same hot story. Within a media system where the marketplace competition has increased over time (as it has in the US), we would likewise expect an increase in the frequency and volatility of media storms over time. We also expect that media systems in countries with more majoritarian governing systems (e.g., two-party systems) will yield media storms with more frequency and volatility, since it is easier in these contexts for potential-media-storm events to be framed in terms of Team A versus Team B competition (Dimitrova and Kostadinova 2013). Beyond these expectations about frequency and volatility of media storms, we have no reason to suspect that our fire triangle model would not apply across democratic contexts. However, it may be the case that the interplay between the three necessary conditions manifests differently. Recall that in the US data we examine here, all the media storms we identified had "High" or "Very High" levels of all three elements (see online appendix for full list). It could be that in other media systems – especially those with less market competition – there exists more of a trade-off between the three elements, such that media storms tend to erupt with only "Medium" or "Medium-High" levels of one or two elements as long as at least one is "Very High." We're excited to see what insights future research unlocks.

We close by noting that although we hope our fire triangle model will be helpful as a theoretical lodestone (or even as a foil) for years to come, the world of political communication is changing fast. For us, writing these final paragraphs in spring of 2025, the most recent media storms in the US included the murder of Brian Thompson, CEO of UnitedHealthcare, in New York City on December 4, 2024; and the heightened international tariffs put into place by the second Trump administration in 2025. Both of these media storms seem to affirm our fire triangle model, while offering intriguing glimpses into the ways in which political communication is, as always, evolving.

Taking the CEO's murder first, the event was high in heat, not only because the murder occurred in cold blood but also because of a string of intriguing facts about the killing, including inscribed cartridge casings left at the scene ("Delay," "Deny," "Depose"), Monopoly money left in a backpack in a nearby park, and partial images of the alleged killer's face showing him to be young and attractive. The event tapped into the fuel of established narratives around Americans' growing frustration with the health care system. And the event received an overwhelming amount of oxygen, some from corporate leaders but mostly on social media, where people tracked the six-day manhunt for the suspect, Luigi Mangione, who was ultimately captured in a McDonald's in Pennsylvania.

Yet the bellows of this social media oxygen were not directed toward the heinousness of Thompson's murder or even the "catch me if you can" intrigue of the manhunt. Rather, the discussion was largely *unsympathetic* to Thompson, dominated by the dark humor of people fed up with the health care industry. Posts included pleas to impede the manhunt (Otis 2024) and a general lack of sympathy for Thompson, including satirical denials of Thompson's would-be medical claim (e.g., "my empathy is out of network" and "[after] a careful review of the claim submitted for emergency services on December 4, 2024 . . . [your claim was denied because] you failed to obtain prior authorization before seeking care for the gunshot wound") (Tufekci 2024). The amount of social media attention (oxygen) in this case was to be expected, given the intrigue of the murder and manhunt. Yet the nature and sentiment of the oxygen is different than anything we have seen before, with the public's reaction seemingly out of sync with American norms of civility and sympathy following a murder.

The media storm surrounding President Trump's tariffs also fits the fire triangle model. The various decisions Trump made in 2025 to increase (and then decrease, then increase . . .) US tariffs on goods from various other countries were inherently newsworthy (heat), affecting not just most people in America but the global economy as well. The notion of tariffs was still front-of-mind (fuel) following the trade wars of Trump's first administration, and the potential effects – good and bad – of the tariffs on everything from the cost of groceries to domestic jobs resonated (more fuel) against the recent economic turbulence of the COVID-19 pandemic and the resulting high inflation that helped Trump get elected in 2024 (Ip 2025). Discussion of the tariffs reverberated well beyond the traditional news media (oxygen), with criticisms coming from international leaders such as Canadian Prime Minister Mark Carney (who won the April 2025 election in large part due to Canadian voters concerned with Trump; Northam 2025), from US companies spanning the auto industry to agriculture, and even from conservative pundits like commentator Ben Shapiro and podcaster Joe Rogan.

This media storm example is striking in at least two ways that we hope prompt additional future research on media storm dynamics: It illustrates the complicated dynamics of storms-within-a-storm, and it suggests that political communication strategies of "flooding the zone" might make these storms-within-a-storm more prevalent. On the storm-within-a-storm idea, empirically the tariff media storm of 2025 was in fact a series of storms within a larger storm. The largest media storm about the tariffs (to date) followed Trump's April 2, 2025, announcement of his long-promised "reciprocal" tariffs, which levied a 10% baseline tax on imports from all countries, as well as higher rates for dozens of other countries. Recalling that our minimum for the media storms we have discussed in this section is 100 news articles (across five key newspapers) in a given week, Trump's April 2 announcement prompted 1,450 articles the following week (up 200% from the 701 articles the previous week, thus easily meeting our change criterion of 150% increase). But the preexisting level of coverage (701 articles in a single week!) was already colossal. The April 2 media storm was simply the latest in a string of media storms about the tariffs, including one triggered by Trump's promise of tariffs during his inauguration speech on January 20, 2025. And even that post-inauguration media storm (453 articles in the first week) occurred against a context of already-high levels of coverage (290 articles the previous week), reaching all the way back to Trump's discussion of tariffs when he was still campaigning (e.g., from August 2024: "Trump, in North Carolina speech, signals openness to expanding tariff plans"; Stein, LeVine, and Arnsdorf 2024). The point is that media coverage of the tariffs had already crept to a new (high) normal, opening the possibility that each storm within the larger storm had greater impact because of the throughline narrative, but also the countervailing possibility that the gravity of each media storm was lost in the shuffle. Even people paying attention to the 2024 election could be forgiven for missing the many stories about Trump's tariff plans and thus being caught off-guard when these plans were realized in 2025.

This notion that Trump's tariff plans were hiding in plain sight brings us to the importance of evolving political communication strategies. Part of the Trump administration's self-described tactic of his second term in office was to "flood the zone" in terms of policy initiatives (Broadwater 2025), but this strategy appears effective in terms of saturating the media agenda space as well (Bordes 2025). This flood-the-zone strategy, combined with a tendency to relish in any media attention, not just positive attention (MacArthur 2025), is a different political approach to interacting with the media than was at play throughout most of the data we have presented here. Within our fire analogy, this political approach brings to mind the term "firestorm": a fire that becomes so intense that it creates and sustains its own wind system. In contexts where such media strategies are in effect, we would expect more of these storms-within-a-storm, with potentially muted effects. Together, these cases remind us that even if our fire triangle model helps predict a future media storm, the underlying workings of the elements are always in flux.

References

A. B. C. News. 2020. "2 Viruses – COVID and Racism – Devastate the Black Community and Threaten America's Stability." https://abcnews.go.com/Politics/viruses-covid-racism-devastate-black-community-threaten-americas/story?id=71016538 (December 22, 2023).

Aeon. 2021. "Coverage of the 'Balloon Boy' Hoax Forms a Withering Indictment of for-Profit News | Aeon Videos." https://aeon.co/videos/coverage-of-the-balloon-boy-hoax-forms-a-withering-indictment-of-for-profit-news (December 19, 2024).

Altman, Alex. 2014. "Person of the Year 2014 Runner-Up: Ferguson Protesters." Time. https://time.com/time-person-of-the-year-runner-up-ferguson-protesters/.

Amster, Sara-Ellen. 2010. "Up, Up and Away: How TV News Blew It." *Huffington Post*. www.huffpost.com/entry/up-up-and-away-how-tv-new_b_329712 (December 23, 2024).

Anderson, Monica, Michael Barthel, Andrew Perrin, and Emily A. Vogels. 2022. "#BlackLivesMatter Surges on Twitter after George Floyd's Death." *Pew Research Center*. www.pewresearch.org/short-reads/2020/06/10/blacklivesmatter-surges-on-twitter-after-george-floyds-death/ (July 24, 2023).

Arango, Tim, Shaila Dewan, and Nicholas Bogel-Burroughs. 2021. "Despite Other Factors, Police Caused Floyd's Death, Medical Examiner Says." *The New York Times*. www.nytimes.com/2021/04/09/us/chauvin-trial-george-floyd-autopsy.html (December 18, 2024).

Arora, Maneesh. 2020. "Analysis | How the Coronavirus Pandemic Helped the Floyd Protests Become the Biggest in U.S. History." *Washington Post*. www.washingtonpost.com/politics/2020/08/05/how-coronavirus-pandemic-helped-floyd-protests-become-biggest-us-history/ (January 20, 2025).

Atkinson, Mary Layton, John Lovett, and Frank R. Baumgartner. 2014. "Measuring the Media Agenda." *Political Communication* 31(2): 355–80. https://doi.org/10.1080/10584609.2013.828139.

Bae, Jin Yung, Evan Anderson, Diana Silver, and James Macinko. 2014. "Child Passenger Safety Laws in the United States, 1978–2010: Policy Diffusion in the Absence of Strong Federal Intervention." *Social Science & Medicine (1982)* 100: 30–37. https://doi.org/10.1016/j.socscimed.2013.10.035.

Baker, Katie J. M. 2016. "Here's The Powerful Letter The Stanford Victim Read To Her Attacker." BuzzFeed News. https://www.buzzfeednews.com/article/katiejmbaker/heres-the-powerful-letter-the-stanford-victim-read-to-her-ra

Ball, Molly. 2023. "How John Fetterman Came Out of the Darkness." *TIME*. https://time.com/6296038/john-fetterman-depression-cover-story/ (November 21, 2024).

Ballard, Heidi L., Emily Evans, Victoria E. Sturtevant, and Pamela Jakes. 2012. "The Evolution of Smokey Bear: Environmental Education about Wildfire for Youth." *The Journal of Environmental Education* 43(4): 227–240.

Bambra, Clare, Julia Lynch, and Katherine E. Smith. 2021. *The Unequal Pandemic: COVID-19 and Health Inequalities*. Bristol: Policy Press. https://doi.org/10.47674/9781447361237.

Baum, Matthew. 2005. *Soft News Goes to War*. Princeton, NJ: Princeton University Press. https://press.princeton.edu/books/paperback/9780691123776/soft-news-goes-to-war (December 21, 2023).

Baumgartner, Frank R., Suzanna L. De Boef, and Amber E. Boydstun. 2008. *The Decline of the Death Penalty and the Discovery of Innocence*. Cambridge: Cambridge University Press.

Baumgartner, Frank R., and Bryan D. Jones. 2009. *Agendas and Instability in American Politics*, 2nd Ed. Chicago, IL: University of Chicago Press. https://press.uchicago.edu/ucp/books/book/chicago/A/bo6763995.html (December 20, 2023).

Bear, Smokey. 2019. "Elements of Fire." https://smokeybear.com/en/about-wildland-fire/fire-science/elements-of-fire (December 18, 2024).

Becker, Amy B. 2012. "Determinants of Public Support for Same-Sex Marriage: Generational Cohorts, Social Contact, and Shifting Attitudes." *International Journal of Public Opinion Research* 24(4): 524–33. https://doi.org/10.1093/ijpor/eds002.

Bennett, W. Lance. 1990. "Toward a Theory of Press-State Relations in the United States." *Journal of Communication* 40(2): 103–25.

Bennett, W. Lance. 2003. "The Burglar Alarm That Just Keeps Ringing: A Response to Zaller." *Political Communication* 20(2): 131–38.

Bergquist, Parrish, and Christopher Warshaw. 2019. "Does Global Warming Increase Public Concern about Climate Change?" *The Journal of Politics* 81(2): 686–91. https://doi.org/10.1086/701766.

Birkland, Thomas A. 1998. "Focusing Events, Mobilization, and Agenda Setting." *Journal of Public Policy* 18(1): 53–74. https://doi.org/10.1017/S0143814X98000038.

Birkland, Thomas A., and Regina G. Lawrence. 2009. "Media Framing and Policy Change after Columbine." *American Behavioral Scientist* 52(10): 1405–25. https://doi.org/10.1177/0002764209332555.

Brody, Debra J., and Qiuping Gu. 2020. "Antidepressant Use Among Adults: United States, 2015-2018." NCHS data brief (377): 1–8.

Bordes, Zoë. 2025. "From Alarm to Overload? Analyzing 'Flooding the Zone' Using the Alarm-Patrol Model of News." University of California, Los Angeles.

Box, G. E. P. 1979. "Robustness in the Strategy of Scientific Model Building." In *Robustness in Statistics*, eds. Robert L. Launer and Graham N. Wilkinson. Cambridge: Academic Press, 201–36. https://doi.org/10.1016/B978-0-12-438150-6.50018-2.

Boydstun, Amber E. 2013. *Making the News: Politics, the Media, and Agenda Setting*. Chicago: The University of Chicago Press.

Boydstun, Amber E., Anne Hardy, and Stefaan Walgrave. 2014. "Two Faces of Media Attention: Media Storm versus Non-Storm Coverage." *Political Communication* 31(4): 509–31. https://doi.org/10.1080/10584609.2013.875967.

Broadwater, Luke. 2025. "Trump's 'Flood the Zone' Strategy Leaves Opponents Gasping in Outrage." *The New York Times*. www.nytimes.com/2025/01/28/us/politics/trump-policy-blitz.html (June 3, 2025).

Brown, Nadia E., Ray Block Jr, and Christopher Stout, eds. 2020. *The Politics of Protest: Readings on the Black Lives Matter Movement*. London: Routledge. https://doi.org/10.4324/9781003119722.

Bump, Philip. 2023. "Analysis | Why Youth Turnout Is a Subplot to Every Election Cycle." *Washington Post*. www.washingtonpost.com/politics/2023/11/08/biden-youth-vote-democrats/ (March 27, 2024).

Cagle, Susie. 2019. "California's Fire Season Has Been Bad: But It Could Have Been Much Worse." *The Guardian*. www.theguardian.com/us-news/2019/nov/01/california-wildfire-season-2019 (July 31, 2023).

Card, Dallas, Amber E. Boydstun, Justin H. Gross, Philip Resnik, and Noah A. Smith. 2015. "The Media Frames Corpus: Annotations of Frames Across Issues." In *Proceedings of the 53rd Annual Meeting of the Association for Computational Linguistics and the 7th International Joint Conference on Natural Language Processing* (Volume 2: Short Papers), Beijing: Association for Computational Linguistics, 438–44. https://doi.org/10.3115/v1/P15-2072.

Chadwick, Andrew. 2017. *The Hybrid Media System: Politics and Power*. 2nd ed. https://academic.oup.com/book/1922 (June 3, 2025).

Chalmers, David M. 1959. "The Muckrakers and the Growth of Corporate Power: A Study in Constructive Journalism." *The American Journal of Economics and Sociology* 18(3): 295–311.

Chapman, Hannah S. 2021. "Shoring Up Autocracy: Participatory Technologies and Regime Support in Putin's Russia." *Comparative Political Studies* 54(8): 1459–89. https://doi.org/10.1177/0010414021989759.

Clarke, Hamish, Brett Cirulis, Trent Penman, Owen Price, Matthias M. Boer, and Ross Bradstock. 2022. "The 2019–2020 Australian Forest Fires Are a Harbinger of Decreased Prescribed Burning Effectiveness under Rising Extreme Conditions." *Scientific Reports* 12(1): 11871. https://doi.org/10.1038/s41598-022-15262-y.

Clayton, Dewey M. 2018. "Black Lives Matter and the Civil Rights Movement: A Comparative Analysis of Two Social Movements in the United States." *Journal of Black Studies* 49(5): 448–80. https://doi.org/10.1177/0021934718764099.

Cowart, Holly S., Ginger E. Blackstone, and Jeffrey K. Riley. 2022. "Framing a Movement: Media Portrayals of the George Floyd Protests on Twitter." *Journalism & Mass Communication Quarterly* 99(3): 676–95. https://doi.org/10.1177/10776990221109232.

van Dalen, Arjen. 2012. "Structural Bias in Cross-National Perspective: How Political Systems and Journalism Cultures Influence Government Dominance in the News." *The International Journal of Press/Politics* 17(1): 32–55. https://doi.org/10.1177/1940161211411087.

Daly, Christopher B. 2012. *Covering America: A Narrative History of a Nation's Journalism*. Amherst: University of Massachusetts Press. https://muse.jhu.edu/pub/190/monograph/book/13662 (June 4, 2025).

Day, Elizabeth. 2015. "#BlackLivesMatter: The Birth of a New Civil Rights Movement." *The Observer*. www.theguardian.com/world/2015/jul/19/blacklivesmatter-birth-civil-rights-movement (January 25, 2025).

Day, Liz, Samantha Stark, and Joe Coscarelli. 2021. "Britney Spears Quietly Pushed for Years to End Her Conservatorship." *The New York Times*. www.nytimes.com/2021/06/22/arts/music/britney-spears-conservatorship.html (December 18, 2024).

Dimitrova, Daniela V., and Petia Kostadinova. 2013. "Identifying Antecedents of the Strategic Game Frame: A Longitudinal Analysis." *Journalism & Mass Communication Quarterly* 90(1): 75–88. https://doi.org/10.1177/1077699012468739.

Douai, Aziz, Mehmet F. Bastug, and Davut Akca. 2022. "Framing Syrian Refugees: US Local News and the Politics of Immigration." *International Communication Gazette* 84(2): 93–112. https://doi.org/10.1177/17480485211006662.

Downs, Anthony. 1972. "Up and Down with Ecology: The 'Issue-Attention Cycle.'" *Public Interest* 28(Summer): 38–50.

Druckman, James N., and Mary C. McGrath. 2019. "The Evidence for Motivated Reasoning in Climate Change Preference Formation." *Nature Climate Change* 9(2): 111–19. https://doi.org/10.1038/s41558-018-0360-1.

Dunivin, Zackary Okun, Harry Yaojun Yan, Jelani Ince, and Fabio Rojas. 2022. "Black Lives Matter Protests Shift Public Discourse." *Proceedings of the*

National Academy of Sciences 119(10): e2117320119. https://doi.org/10.1073/pnas.2117320119.

Echelon Insights. 2014. "#TheYearInNews 2014." https://echeloninsights.tumblr.com/post/105911206078/theyearinnews-2014 (December 4, 2025).

Farhi, Paul, and Sarah Ellison. 2020. "Ignited by Public Protests, American Newsrooms Are Having Their Own Racial Reckoning." *Washington Post*. www.washingtonpost.com/lifestyle/media/ignited-by-public-protests-american-newsrooms-are-having-their-own-racial-reckoning/2020/06/12/be622bce-a995-11ea-94d2-d7bc43b26bf9_story.html (December 20, 2024).

Farooq, Umar. 2024. "Body Cameras Were Sold as a Tool for Police Reform: Ten Years Later, Most Footage Is Kept from Public View." *The Current*. http://thecurrentga.org/2024/01/10/body-cameras-were-sold-as-a-tool-for-police-reform-ten-years-later-most-footage-is-kept-from-public-view/ (December 23, 2024).

Fleur, Nicholas St. 2015. "The Science Behind the Dress." *The New York Times*. www.nytimes.com/2015/05/15/science/the-science-behind-the-dress-color.html (December 18, 2024).

Folkenflik, David. 2022. "A Rape, an Abortion, and a One-Source Story: A Child's Ordeal Becomes National News." *NPR*. www.npr.org/2022/07/13/1111285143/abortion-10-year-old-raped-ohio (December 18, 2024).

Ford, Jessica L., Matthew Douglas, and Ashley K. Barrett. 2023. "The Role of Pandemic Fatigue in Seeking and Avoiding Information on COVID-19 among Young Adults." *Health Communication* 38(11): 2336–49. https://doi.org/10.1080/10410236.2022.2069211.

Fowler, Geoffrey A. 2020. "Perspective | Black Lives Matter Could Change Facial Recognition Forever – If Big Tech Doesn't Stand in the Way." *Washington Post*. www.washingtonpost.com/technology/2020/06/12/facial-recognition-ban/ (January 21, 2025).

Galtung, Johan, and Mari Holmboe Ruge. 1965. "The Structure of Foreign News: The Presentation of the Congo, Cuba and Cyprus Crises in Four Norwegian Newspapers." *Journal of Peace Research* 2(1): 64–90. https://doi.org/10.1177/002234336500200104.

Gammon, Katharine. 2018. "New Data Show the NRA Increased Online Ad Spending Aggressively after Parkland Shooting – Chicago Tribune." www.chicagotribune.com/business/blue-sky/sns-tns-bc-guns-kids-advertising-20180323-story.html (February 1, 2023).

Gans, Herbert J. 2004. *Deciding What's News: A Study of CBS Evening News, NBC Nightly News, Newsweek, and Time*. Northwestern University Press.

Garcia, Sandra E. 2017. "The Woman Who Created #MeToo Long before Hashtags." *The New York Times*. www.nytimes.com/2017/10/20/us/me-too-movement-tarana-burke.html (December 19, 2023).

Goldsby, Jacqueline. 1996. "The High and Low Tech of It: The Meaning of Lynching and the Death of Emmett Till." *The Yale Journal of Criticism* 9(2): 245–82.

Goodman, Amy. 2015. "Ta-Nehisi Coates on Police Brutality: 'The Violence Is Not New, It's the Cameras That Are New.'" Democracy Now! http://www.democracynow.org/2015/9/7/ta_nehisi_coates_on_police_brutality (November 12, 2025).

Goyanes, Manuel, Alberto Ardèvol-Abreu, and Homero Gil De Zúñiga. 2023. "Antecedents of News Avoidance: Competing Effects of Political Interest, News Overload, Trust in News Media, and 'News Finds Me' Perception." *Digital Journalism* 11(1): 1–18. https://doi.org/10.1080/21670811.2021.1990097.

Granovetter, Mark. 1978. "Threshold Models of Collective Behavior." *American Journal of Sociology* 83(6): 1420–43.

Gruszczynski, Mike. 2020. "How Media Storms and Topic Diversity Influence Agenda Fragmentation." *International Journal of Communication* 14(0): 22.

Gupta, Arun. 2024. "Students for Gaza Are Undeterred -." *YES! Magazine Journalism*. www.yesmagazine.org/opinion/2024/05/16/students-gaza-columbia (December 19, 2024).

Gurr, Gwendolin, and Julia Metag. 2022. "Fatigued by Ongoing News Issues? How Repeated Exposure to the Same News Issue Affects the Audience." *Mass Communication and Society* 25(4): 578–99. https://doi.org/10.1080/15205436.2021.1956543.

Gutman, Abraham, and Dylan Purcell. 2023. "A U.S. Senator Openly Seeking Treatment for Mental Health Is Rare. So Is Staying 44 Days in a Pa. Hospital for Depression." *The Philadelphia Inquirer*. www.inquirer.com/health/john-fetterman-senator-depression-treatment-health-20230417.html (December 21, 2023).

Haider-Markel, Donald P., William Delehanty, and Matthew Beverlin. 2007. "Media Framing and Racial Attitudes in the Aftermath of Katrina." *Policy Studies Journal* 35(4): 587–605. https://doi.org/10.1111/j.1541-0072.2007.00238.x.

Hallin, Daniel, and Paolo Mancini. 2004. *Comparing Media Systems: Three Models of Media and Politics*. New York: Cambridge University Press. https://app.readcube.com/library/5506c919-d67b-4a83-be75-fb5a55200fc2/item/d40e2833-c199-4c6f-a39b-851add251c51.

Harcup, Tony, and Deirdre O'neill. 2001. "What Is News? Galtung and Ruge Revisited." *Journalism Studies* 2, 261-280. https://doi.org/10.1080/14616700118449

Harcup, Tony, and Deirdre O'neill. 2017. "What Is News? News Values Revisited (Again)." *Journalism Studies* 18(12): 1470–88.

Healy, Jack. 2014. "Up Early and in Line for a Marijuana Milestone in Colorado." The New York Times. https://www.nytimes.com/2014/01/02/us/colorado-stores-throw-open-their-doors-to-pot-buyers.html.

Hill, Benjamin Mako. 2013. "Almost Wikipedia: Eight Early Encyclopedia Projects and the Mechanisms of Collective Action." Massachusetts Institute of Technology.

Hooker, Juliet. 2023. *Black Grief/White Grievance*. Princeton, NJ: Princeton University Press. https://press.princeton.edu/books/hardcover/9780691243030/black-griefwhite-grievance (December 21, 2023).

Horsley, Scott. 2020. "From Jobs to Homeownership, Protests Put Spotlight on Racial Economic Divide." *NPR*. www.npr.org/2020/06/01/866794025/from-jobs-to-homeownership-protests-put-spotlight-on-economic-divide (December 20, 2023).

Houston, J. Brian, Betty Pfefferbaum, and Cathy Ellen Rosenholtz. 2012. "Disaster News: Framing and Frame Changing in Coverage of Major U.S. Natural Disasters, 2000–2010." *Journalism & Mass Communication Quarterly* 89(4): 606–23. https://doi.org/10.1177/1077699012456022.

Huang, Yi-Hui. 2006. "Crisis Situations, Communication Strategies, and Media Coverage: A Multicase Study Revisiting the Communicative Response Model." *Communication Research* 33(3): 180–205. https://doi.org/10.1177/0093650206287077.

Hunt, Kate. 2022. "Exploiting a Crisis: Abortion Activism and the COVID-19 Pandemic." *Perspectives on Politics* 20(2): 396–411. https://doi.org/10.1017/S1537592720004673.

Inskeep, Steve, and Noel King. 2020. "News Brief: Protests Over George Floyd's Death Show No Signs of Letting Up." *NPR*. www.npr.org/2020/06/01/866540157/morning-news-brief (December 20, 2023).

Ip, Greg. 2025. "Inflation Helped Trump Get Elected: Now It's His Problem." *WSJ*. www.wsj.com/economy/inflation-helped-trump-get-elected-now-its-his-problem-87e995e3 (June 4, 2025).

Iyengar, Shanto. 1991. *Is Anyone Responsible? How Television Frames Political Issues*. Chicago, IL: University of Chicago Press.

Jacobs, Alan M., J. Scott Matthews, Timothy Hicks, and Eric Merkley. 2021. "Whose News? Class-Biased Economic Reporting in the United States." *American Political Science Review* 115(3): 1016–33. https://doi.org/10.1017/S0003055421000137.

Jacobs, Laura, and Joost Van Spanje. 2023. "Gatekeeping, News Values and Selection: Factors Determining the Newsworthiness of Hate Crimes."

Journalism Studies 24(13): 1692–710. https://doi.org/10.1080/1461670X.2023.2246076.

Johann, Michael. 2022. "Political Participation in Transition: Internet Memes as a Form of Political Expression in Social Media." *Studies in Communication Sciences* 22(1): 149–64. https://doi.org/10.24434/j.scoms.2022.01.3005.

Johnson, Thaddeus L., and Natasha N. Johnson. 2020. "Police Facial Recognition Technology Can't Tell Black People Apart." *Scientific American*. www.scientificamerican.com/article/police-facial-recognition-technology-cant-tell-black-people-apart/ (January 21, 2025).

Kealy, Courtney. 2021. "A Decade on, Occupy Wall Street's Legacy on Income Inequality." *Al Jeezera*. www.aljazeera.com/economy/2021/9/17/a-decade-on-occupy-wall-streets-legacy-on-income-inequality (January 21, 2025).

Keating, Dan. 2022. "Guns Killed More Young People than Cars Did for the First Time in 2020." *Washington Post*. www.washingtonpost.com/health/2022/05/25/guns-kill-more-kids-than-cars/ (July 31, 2023).

Kent, Stephen A. 2001. *From Slogans to Mantras: Social Protest and Religious Conversion in the Late Vietnam War Era*. New York: Syracuse University Press.

Kepplinger, Hans Mathias, Hans-Bernd Brosius, and Joachim Friedrich Staab. 1991. "Instrumental Actualization: A Theory of Mediated Conflicts." *European Journal of Communication* 6(3): 263–90. https://doi.org/10.1177/0267323191006003002.

Kingdon, John W. 2010. *Agendas, Alternatives, and Public Policies*. 2nd Ed. New York: Pearson.

Kotcher, John, Lauren Feldman, Kate T. Luong, James Wyatt, and Edward Maibach. 2021. "Advocacy Messages about Climate and Health Are More Effective When They Include Information about Risks, Solutions, and a Normative Appeal: Evidence from a Conjoint Experiment." *The Journal of Climate Change and Health* 3: 100030. https://doi.org/10.1016/j.joclim.2021.100030.

Laurencin, Cato T., and Joanne M. Walker. 2020. "A Pandemic on a Pandemic: Racism and COVID-19 in Blacks." *Cell Systems* 11(1): 9–10. https://doi.org/10.1016/j.cels.2020.07.002.

Lawrence, Regina G. 2022. *The Politics of Force: Media and the Construction of Police Brutality*. Updated Edition. Oxford: Oxford University Press.

Lawrence, Regina G., and Thomas A. Birkland. 2004. "Guns, Hollywood, and School Safety: Defining the School-Shooting Problem Across Public Arenas*." *Social Science Quarterly* 85(5): 1193–207. https://doi.org/10.1111/j.0038-4941.2004.00271.x.

Lazer, David M. J., Matthew A. Baum, Yochai Benkler, Adam J. Berinsky, Kelly M. Greenhill, Filippo Menczer, Miriam J. Metzger, Brendan Nyhan, Gordon Pennycook, David Rothschild, Michael Schudson, Steven A. Sloman, Cass R. Sunstein, Emily A. Thorson, Duncan J. Watts, and Jonathan L. Zittrain. 2018. "The Science of Fake News." *Science* 359(6380): 1094–96. https://doi.org/10.1126/science.aao2998.

Lee, Nicol Turner. 2020. "Where Would Racial Progress in Policing Be without Camera Phones?" *Brookings*. www.brookings.edu/articles/where-would-racial-progress-in-policing-be-without-camera-phones/ (December 18, 2024).

Litterer, Benjamin, David Jurgens, and Dallas Card. 2023. "When It Rains, It Pours: Modeling Media Storms and the News Ecosystem." In *Findings of the Association for Computational Linguistics: EMNLP 2023*, eds. Houda Bouamor, Juan Pino, and Kalika Bali. Singapore: Association for Computational Linguistics, 6346–61. https://doi.org/10.18653/v1/2023.findings-emnlp.420.

Lum, Cynthia, Megan Stoltz, Christopher S. Koper, and J. Amber Scherer. 2019. "Research on Body-Worn Cameras." *Criminology & Public Policy* 18(1): 93–118. https://doi.org/10.1111/1745-9133.12412.

MacArthur, John R. 2025. "Trump Isn't a Narcissist – He's a Solipsist." *The Guardian*. www.theguardian.com/commentisfree/2025/feb/08/donald-trump-media-coverage (June 3, 2025).

Maloy, J. S. 2020. "Political Realism as Anti-Scholastic Practice: Methodological Lessons from Muckraking Journalism." *Political Research Quarterly* 73(1): 27–39. https://doi.org/10.1177/1065912919873973.

Mazumder, Soumyajit. 2018. "The Persistent Effect of U.S. Civil Rights Protests on Political Attitudes." *American Journal of Political Science* 62(4): 922–35.

McAdam, Doug. 2017. "Social Movement Theory and the Prospects for Climate Change Activism in the United States." *Annual Review of Political Science* 20(1): 189–208.https://doi.org/10.1146/annurev-polisci-052615-025801.

McCombs, Maxwell, and Donald L Shaw. 1972. "The Agenda-Setting Function of Mass Media." *Public Opinion Quarterly* 36(2): 176–87.

McVicker, Stephanie M. 2021. ProQuest Dissertations and Theses "Political Disinformation, Propaganda, and Persuasion in Memes: A Content Analysis of 2020 U.S. Election Political Memes." Ph.D. Robert Morris University. www.proquest.com/docview/2596288007/abstract/F2748B2CA8904788PQ/1 (November 7, 2022).

Minutaglio, Rose. 2019. "Capt. Sully on the Ten Year Anniversary of 'Miracle' Landing on Hudson River." *Esquire*. www.esquire.com/news-politics/

a25838404/captain-sully-sullenberger-miracle-landing-ten-year-anniversary-interview/ (December 18, 2024).
Monmouth. 2020. "Protestors' Anger Justified Even if Actions May Not Be." *Monmouth University Polling Institute*. www.monmouth.edu/polling-institute/reports/monmouthpoll_us_060220/ (December 18, 2024).
Montpetit, Éric, and Alexandre Harvey. 2018. "Media Storms and Policy Expertise: How Environmental Beat Journalists Gained Influence during a Shale Gas Controversy." *Environmental Communication* 12(7): 895–910. https://doi.org/10.1080/17524032.2018.1495092.
Mortensen, Mette, and Christina Neumayer. 2021. "The Playful Politics of Memes." *Information, Communication & Society* 24(16): 2367–77. https://doi.org/10.1080/1369118X.2021.1979622.
Moyles, Sarah. 2017. "A Timeline of the Syrian Civil War and Refugee Crisis." *UNICEF Ireland*. www.unicef.ie/stories/timeline-syrian-war-refugee-crisis/ (July 31, 2023).
NCSL. 2021. *Body-Worn Camera Laws Database*. National Conference of State Legislatures. www.ncsl.org/civil-and-criminal-justice/body-worn-camera-laws-database (December 18, 2024).
Neuman, W. Russell. 1990. "The Threshold of Public Attention." *Public Opinion Quarterly* 54(2): 159–76. https://doi.org/10.1086/269194.
Newman, Benjamin J., and Todd K. Hartman. 2019. "Mass Shootings and Public Support for Gun Control." *British Journal of Political Science* 49(4): 1527–53. https://doi.org/10.1017/S0007123417000333.
Newman, Benjamin, Jennifer L. Merolla, Sono Shah et al. 2021. "The Trump Effect: An Experimental Investigation of the Emboldening Effect of Racially Inflammatory Elite Communication." *British Journal of Political Science* 51(3): 1138–59. https://doi.org/10.1017/S0007123419000590.
Nixon, Rob. 2011. *Slow Violence and the Environmentalism of the Poor*. Cambridge: Harvard University Press. https://doi.org/10.2307/j.ctt2jbsgw.
Northam, Jackie. 2025. "Mark Carney Won Canada's Election after a Campaign Dominated by Trump." *NPR*. www.npr.org/2025/04/29/nx-s1-5380765/mark-carney-won-canadas-election-after-a-campaign-dominated-by-trump (June 1, 2025).
Nyhan, Brendan. 2015. "Scandal Potential: How Political Context and News Congestion Affect the President's Vulnerability to Media Scandal." *British Journal of Political Science* 45(2): 435–66.
Otis, Joshua Chaffin, and Ginger Adams. 2024. "Manhunt for UnitedHealthcare CEO Killer Meets Unexpected Obstacle: Sympathy for the Gunman." *Wall Street Journal*. www.wsj.com/us-news/manhunt-for-unitedhealthcare-ceo-

killer-meets-unexpected-obstacle-sympathy-for-the-gunman-31276307 (December 21, 2024).

Pacheco, Julianna. 2012. "The Social Contagion Model: Exploring the Role of Public Opinion on the Diffusion of Antismoking Legislation across the American States." *The Journal of Politics* 74(1): 187–202. https://doi.org/10.1017/S0022381611001241.

Peters, Chris, and Stuart Allan. 2022. "Weaponizing Memes: The Journalistic Mediation of Visual Politicization." *Digital Journalism* 10(2): 217–29. https://doi.org/10.1080/21670811.2021.1903958.

Pew Research Center. 2013. "News Coverage Conveys Strong Momentum for Same-Sex Marriage." www.pewresearch.org/journalism/2013/06/17/news-coverage-conveys-strong-momentum/.

Pew Research Center. 2019. "Attitudes on Same-Sex Marriage." www.pewresearch.org/religion/fact-sheet/changing-attitudes-on-gay-marriage/ (January 21, 2025).

Ploughman, Penelope. 1995. "The American Print News Media 'Construction' of Five Natural Disasters." *Disasters* 19(4): 308–26. https://doi.org/10.1111/j.1467-7717.1995.tb00352.x.

Prabha, Chandra, Lynn Silipigni Connaway, Lawrence Olszewski, and Lillie R. Jenkins. 2007. "What Is Enough? Satisficing Information Needs." *Journal of Documentation* 63(1): 74–89. https://doi.org/10.1108/00220410710723894.

Price, Jessica Taylor. 2022. "More Children Died from Gun Violence than Car Crashes: Are School Shootings to Blame?" *Northeastern Global News*. https://news.northeastern.edu/2022/06/03/children-gun-violence/ (December 21, 2023).

Raguso, Emilie. 2019. "UC Berkeley Student Charged with Sexual Assaults Ordered to Stand Trial." *Berkeleyside*. www.berkeleyside.org/2019/09/17/uc-berkeley-student-charged-with-sexual-assaults-ordered-to-trial (November 21, 2024).

Reny, Tyler T., and Benjamin J. Newman. 2021. "The Opinion-Mobilizing Effect of Social Protest against Police Violence: Evidence from the 2020 George Floyd Protests." *American Political Science Review* 115(4): 1499–507. https://doi.org/10.1017/S0003055421000460.

Roberts, Frank Leon. 2018. *How Black Lives Matter Changed the Way Americans Fight for Freedom*. American Civil Liberties Union (ACLU). www.aclu.org/news/racial-justice/how-black-lives-matter-changed-way-americans-fight (December 18, 2024).

Rogowski, Jon C., and Patrick D. Tucker. 2019. "Critical Events and Attitude Change: Support for Gun Control After Mass Shootings."

Political Science Research and Methods 7(4): 903–11. https://doi.org/10.1017/psrm.2018.21.

Rouf, Khadj, and Tony Wainwright. 2020. "Linking Health Justice, Social Justice, and Climate Justice." *The Lancet Planetary Health* 4(4): e131–32. https://doi.org/10.1016/S2542-5196(20)30083-8.

Sadiki, Larbi, and Layla Saleh. 2023. "Crisis of Democratisation in the Maghreb and North Africa." *The Journal of North African Studies* 28(6): 317–1323.

Schattschneider, E. E. 1960. *The Semisovereign People: A Realist's View of Democracy in America*. New York: Holt, Rinehart and Winston.

Schmuck, Desirée, Raffael Heiss, Jörg Matthes, Sven Engesser, and Frank Esser. 2017. "Antecedents of Strategic Game Framing in Political News Coverage." *Journalism* 18(8): 937–55. https://doi.org/10.1177/1464884916648098.

Schwartz, Gabriel L., and Jaquelyn L. Jahn. 2020. "Mapping Fatal Police Violence across U.S. Metropolitan Areas: Overall Rates and Racial/Ethnic Inequities, 2013–2017." *PLOS ONE* 15(6): e0229686. https://doi.org/10.1371/journal.pone.0229686.

Searles, Kathleen, and Kevin K. Banda. 2019. "But Her Emails! How Journalistic Preferences Shaped Election Coverage in 2016." *Journalism* 20(8): 1052–69. https://doi.org/10.1177/1464884919845459.

Shackford, Scott. 2016. "Americans Overwhelmingly Support Police Body Cameras, Understand They're for Both Sides." *Reason.com*. https://reason.com/2016/01/05/americans-overwhelmingly-support-police/ (December 18, 2024).

Shipan, Charles R., and Craig Volden. 2008. "The Mechanisms of Policy Diffusion." *American Journal of Political Science* 52(4): 840–57. https://doi.org/10.1111/j.1540-5907.2008.00346.x.

von Sikorski, Christian. 2017. "Politische Skandalberichterstattung: ein Forschungsüberblick und Systematisierungsversuch." *Publizistik* 62(3): 299–323. https://doi.org/10.1007/s11616-017-0355-3.

Simpson, Grace. 2024. "The Militarization of Policing in the United States." *The Mid-Southern Journal of Criminal Justice* 23(1). https://mds.marshall.edu/msjcj/vol23/iss1/3.

Skovsgaard, Morten, and Kim Andersen. 2020. "Conceptualizing News Avoidance: Towards a Shared Understanding of Different Causes and Potential Solutions." *Journalism Studies* 21(4): 459–76. https://doi.org/10.1080/1461670X.2019.1686410.

Slakoff, Danielle C., and Henry F. Fradella. 2019. "Media Messages Surrounding Missing Women and Girls: The 'Missing White Woman Syndrome' and Other

Factors That Influence Newsworthiness." *Criminology, Criminal Justice, Law & Society* 20(3): 80–102.

Soroka, Stuart, and Yanna Krupnikov. 2021. *The Increasing Viability of Good News*. Cambridge: Cambridge University Press. https://doi.org/10.1017/9781108982375.

Staab, Joachim Friedrich. 1990. "The Role of News Factors in News Selection: A Theoretical Reconsideration." *European Journal of Communication* 5(4): 423–43. https://doi.org/10.1177/0267323190005004003.

Staff. 2020. "Ahmaud Arbery's Parents Call for Arrests after 'Modern Lynching in the Middle of the Day.'" *The Guardian*. www.theguardian.com/us-news/2020/may/07/ahmaud-arbery-parents-call-for-arrests-killing-song-daily-jog (December 21, 2023).

Stein, Jeff, Marianne LeVine, and Isaac Arnsdorf. 2024. "Trump, in North Carolina Speech, Signals Openness to Expanding Tariff Plans." *The Washington Post*. www.washingtonpost.com/politics/2024/08/14/trump-rally-speech-north-carolina-economy-jd-vance/ (June 1, 2025).

Stelter, Brian. 2012. "In Slain Teenager's Case, a Long Route to National Attention." *The New York Times*. www.nytimes.com/2012/03/26/business/media/for-martins-case-a-long-route-to-national-attention.html (January 15, 2025).

Tewksbury, David, Michelle L. Hals, and Allyson Bibart. 2008. "The Efficacy of News Browsing: The Relationship of News Consumption Style to Social and Political Efficacy." *Journalism & Mass Communication Quarterly* 85(2): 257–72. https://doi.org/10.1177/107769900808500203.

"The Cost of Fire: An Economic Analysis of Indonesia's 2015 Fire Crisis." *World Bank*. https://documents.worldbank.org/pt/publication/documents-reports/documentdetail/776101467990969768/The-cost-of-fire-an-economic-analysis-of-Indonesia-s-2015-fire-crisis (July 31, 2023).

The Drum. 2020. "Twitter: Twitter Black Lives Matter Billboards." *Creative Works*. www.thedrum.com/creative-works/project/twitter-twitter-black-lives-matter-billboards (January 25, 2025).

Tufekci, Zeynep. 2024. "Opinion | The Rage and Glee That Followed a C.E.O.'s Killing Should Ring All Alarms." *The New York Times*. www.nytimes.com/2024/12/06/opinion/united-health-care-ceo-shooting.html (December 21, 2024).

Usher, Nik, and Jessica C. Hagman. 2025. *Amplifying Extremism: Small Town Politicians, Media Storms, and American Journalism*. New York: Cambridge University Press.

Van De Velde, Cécile. 2022. "The Power of Slogans: Using Protest Writings in Social Movement Research." *Social Movement Studies* 23(5): 569–588. https://doi.org/10.1080/14742837.2022.2084065.

Vasterman, Peter L. M. 2005. "Media-Hype: Self-Reinforcing News Waves, Journalistic Standards and the Construction of Social Problems." *European Journal of Communication* 20(4): 508–30. https://doi.org/10.1177/0267323105058254.

Vasterman, Peter, Adam Auch, Audun Beyer et al. 2018. *From Media Hype to Twitter Storm: News Explosions and Their Impact on Issues, Crises and Public Opinion*. Amsterdam: Amsterdam University Press. https://doi.org/10.5117/9789462982178.

Walgrave, Stefaan, Amber E. Boydstun, Rens Vliegenthart, and Anne Hardy. 2017. "The Nonlinear Effect of Information on Political Attention: Media Storms and U.S. Congressional Hearings." *Political Communication* 34(4): 548–70. https://doi.org/10.1080/10584609.2017.1289288.

Walters, Patrick. 2022. "Reclaiming Control: How Journalists Embrace Social Media Logics While Defending Journalistic Values." *Digital Journalism* 10(9): 1482–1501. https://doi.org/10.1080/21670811.2021.1942113.

Weaver, David H., and Lars Willnat. 2016. "Changes in U.S. Journalism: How Do Journalists Think about Social Media?" *Journalism Practice* 10(7): 844–55. https://doi.org/10.1080/17512786.2016.1171162.

White, Arica. 2021. "Addressing Racial and Ethnic Disparities in COVID-19 among School-Aged Children: Are We Doing Enough?" *Preventing Chronic Disease* 18. https://doi.org/10.5888/pcd18.210084.

Wien, Charlotte, and Christian Elmelund-Præstekær. 2009. "An Anatomy of Media Hypes: Developing a Model for the Dynamics and Structure of Intense Media Coverage of Single Issues." *European Journal of Communication* 24(2): 183–201. https://doi.org/10.1177/0267323108101831.

Wiener, Jocelyn. 2021. "The Britney Effect: How California Is Grappling with Conservatorship." *CalMatters*. http://calmatters.org/justice/2021/07/britney-spears-conservatorship/

Yangfang, Tan. 2012. "A Review of the 'Occupy Wall Street' Movement and Its Global Influence." *International Critical Thought* 2(2): 247–54.

Yokum, David, Anita Ravishankar, and Alexander Coppock. 2019. "A Randomized Control Trial Evaluating the Effects of Police Body-Worn Cameras." *Proceedings of the National Academy of Sciences* 116(21): 10329–32. https://doi.org/10.1073/pnas.1814773116.

Young, Gregory, and Mateusz Leszczynski. 2021. In *Revolutions: Theorists, Theory and Practice*, eds. Gregory Young and Mateusz Leszczynski. Colorado Pressbooks Network. "American Revolutions? The Left/Occupy Wall Street and Black Lives Matter." https://colorado.pressbooks.pub/revolution/chapter/american-revolutions-the-left-occupy-wall-street-and-black-lives-matter/ (December 20, 2024).

Zai, Florin. n.d. "From Spark to Scandal: Media Dynamics in the Coverage of Political Failure." University of Fribourg.

Zaller, John. 2003. "A New Standard of News Quality: Burglar Alarms for the Monitorial Citizen." *Political Communication* 20(2): 109–30. https://doi.org/10.1080/10584600390211136.

Acknowledgments

This Element would not exist without a phenomenal team of research assistants. They did much more than execute assigned tasks. They brought fresh curiosity and insights that enriched the work beyond measure. There are many people in this list, having spanned multiple cohorts of research labs, but we are grateful to each and every one: Eden Ackrich, Saloni Agarwal, Ana Bach, Jacob Bentham, Allison Berkowitz, Lucas Bermejo, Laura Bodre, Aaron Bonner, Ellie Bono, Noreen Brar, Oliver Bublitz, Clare Callahan, Nicolle Chase, Sarah Cleary, Corey Coates, Kristine Craig, Roy Crumrine, Jason Cummings, Dominic Faria, Kacey Fifield, Mia Golden, Anish Gopala, Shayla Griffin, Iniyizh Hariharan, Jordan Harris, Deanna Hernandez, Kaleigh Homstad, Scott Huffard, Nicholas Jensen, Abigail Johnson, Meher Khandpur, Marc Kildare, Jeremy Kirshner, Kyle Knight, Meghana Kotha, Anna Kraemer, Emily Lahl, Olivia Lanvi Tran, Alex Lee, Matthew Lesenyie, Danielle Levin, Shoshana Levy, Adrian Lopez, Gloire Mahoro, Spencer McManus, Kylie Mendoca, Summer Mielke, Brandon Miller, Kristen Millstein, Jessicca Mosack, Hannah Dillman Murnane, Andrea Nicolau, McKenna Nolan, Chiamaka Ogumana, Amazing-Grace Olatunji, Lei Otsuka, Samantha Parr, Haining Peng, Sabrina Pertica, Claire Rapp, Bella Richmond, Olivia Rockeman, Mauricio Romero, Caroline Rutten, Jake Ryan, Olivia Sample, Dana Scott, Ramapriya Setty, Nahima Shaffer, Xaria Shephard, Daniel Shuster, Gareth Smythe, Kyle Snowden, Griffin Sproul, Sena Tamene, Ritu Thirunahari, Molly Thompson, Enes Topcu, Ritama Vallishayee, Kristina Victor, Francheska Vincents, Jack Wang, Miki Wayne, Matthew Weber, Andrew Williams, Eden Jade Wolansky, Emelia Yang, Sum-Yee Yek, Sabrina Younes, Priscilla Zambrano, Sunny Zhou, and Hadeel Zidan.

We are especially thankful to Cassie Gorman, who served as our fearless and innovative lab leader during the most critical phases of the project and who consistently inspired us to think about the work in a new light.

We are also grateful for the astute and kind insight offered by colleagues including Scott Althaus, Frank Baumgartner, Shaun Bevan, Derek Epp, Jessica Feezell, Rebecca Glazier, Christoffer Green-Pedersen, Emiliano Grossman, Allison Harell, Jennifer Jerit, Anissa Joseph, Regina Lawrence, Beth Leech, Jamie Monogan, Nik Usher, Stefaan Walgrave, and Florin Zai, as well as the students in FRS 4 and POL 290a. Special thanks to Stuart Soroka for championing this Element, start to finish.

This research was made possible by a National Science Foundation Grant (No. IIS-1211266, to A.E.B. and No. IIS-1211277 to N.A.S.), a Natural

Sciences and Engineering Research Council of Canada Postgraduate Scholarship (to D.C.), a Bloomberg Data Science Research Grant (to A.E.B. and N.A.S.), a University of Washington Innovation Award (to N.A.S.), and a Rapoport Family Foundation Fellowship (to J.R.L.).

Finally, we thank our families for their seemingly endless patience and support. For Amber: Mom, Dad, Kelly, Eric, Siiri, and Margaret. For Jill: Mike, Sloane, Dad and Sandi, Mom, and my sisters, Sarah and Andrea. For Dallas: all my family and friends. For Noah: Karen.

Politics and Communication

Stuart Soroka
University of California, Los Angeles

Stuart Soroka is a Professor in the Departments of Communication and Political Science at the University of California, Los Angeles. His research focuses on political communication, political psychology, and the relationships between public policy, public opinion and mass media. His books with Cambridge University Press include *Information and Democracy* (2022, with Christopher Wlezien), The Increasing Viability of Good News (2021, with Yanna Krupnikov), Negativity in Democratic Politics (2014), and Degrees of Democracy (2010, with Christopher Wlezien).

About the Series

Cambridge Elements in Politics and Communication publishes research focused on the intersection of media, technology, and politics. The series emphasizes forward-looking reviews of the field, path-breaking theoretical and methodological innovations, and the timely application of social-scientific theory and methods to current developments in politics and communication around the world.

Cambridge Elements

Politics and Communication

Elements in the Series

Economic News: Antecedents and Effects
Rens Vliegenthart, Alyt Damstra, Mark Boukes and Jeroen Jonkman

The Increasing Viability of Good News
Stuart Soroka and Yanna Krupnikov

Digital Transformations of the Public Arena
Andreas Jungherr and Ralph Schroeder

Battleground: Asymmetric Communication Ecologies and the Erosion of Civil Society in Wisconsin
Lewis A. Friedland, Dhavan V. Shah, Michael W. Wagner, Katherine J. Cramer, Chris Wells and Jon Pevehouse

Constructing Political Expertise in the News
Kathleen Searles, Yanna Krupnikov, John Barry Ryan and Hillary Style

The YouTube Apparatus
Kevin Munger

How News Coverage of Misinformation Shapes Perceptions and Trust
Emily Thorson

Angry and Wrong: The Emotional Dynamics of Partisan Media and Political Misperceptions
Brian E. Weeks

Social Media Democracy Mirage: How Social Media News Fuels a Politically Uninformed Participatory Democracy
Homero Gil de Zúñiga, Hugo Marcos-Marne, Manuel Goyanes and Rebecca Scheffauer

Political Representation as Communicative Practice
Fabio Wolkenstein and Christopher Wratil

Amplifying Extremism: Small Town Politicians, Media Storms, and American Journalism
Nik Usher and Jessica C. Hagman

Catching Fire in the News: The Necessary Conditions for Media Storms
Amber E. Boydstun, Jill R. Laufer, Dallas Card, Noah A. Smith

A full series listing is available at: www.cambridge.org/EPCM

For EU product safety concerns, contact us at Calle de José Abascal, 56–1°, 28003 Madrid, Spain or eugpsr@cambridge.org.

www.ingramcontent.com/pod-product-compliance
Lightning Source LLC
LaVergne TN
LVHW011849060526
838200LV00054B/4241